I0659462

HAUNTING HANDS

STUDIES IN MOBILE COMMUNICATION

Studies in Mobile Communication focuses on the social consequences of mobile communication in society.

Series Editors

Rich Ling, *Nanyang Technological University, Singapore*
Gerard Goggin, *University of Sydney, Australia*
Leopoldina Fortunati, *Università di Udine, Italy*

Haunting Hands: Mobile Media Practices and Loss
Kathleen M. Cumiskey and Larissa Hjorth

HAUNTING HANDS

Mobile Media Practices and Loss

Kathleen M. Cumiskey and Larissa Hjorth

OXFORD
UNIVERSITY PRESS

OXFORD

UNIVERSITY PRESS

Oxford University Press is a department of the University of Oxford. It furthers the University's objective of excellence in research, scholarship, and education by publishing worldwide. Oxford is a registered trade mark of Oxford University Press in the UK and certain other countries.

Published in the United States of America by Oxford University Press
198 Madison Avenue, New York, NY 10016, United States of America.

Library of Congress Cataloging-in-Publication Data
Names: Cumiskey, Kathleen M.,
1970- author. | Hjorth, Larissa, author.
Title: Haunting hands : mobile media practices and loss / Kathleen M. Cumiskey,
Larissa Hjorth.
Description: New York, NY : Oxford University Press, [2017] | Includes
bibliographical references and index.Identifiers: LCCN 2016038868 (print) |
LCCN 2016052755 (ebook) | ISBN 9780190634988 (pbk. : alk. paper) |
ISBN 9780190634971 (cloth : alk. paper) | ISBN 9780190634995 (pdf) |
ISBN 9780190635008 (online course)Subjects: LCSH:
Information technology—Social aspects. | Mobile communication
systems—Social aspects. | Cell phones—Social aspects. | Loss (Psychology) |
Mass media and culture. | Information society. Classification:
LCC HM851 .C866 2017 (print) | LCC HM851 (ebook) |
DDC 303.48/33—dc23
LC record available at https://lccn.loc.gov/2016038868

Life changes in the instant. The ordinary instant.

—Joan Didion, The Year of Magical Thinking

CONTENTS

LIST OF FIGURES

ACKNOWLEDGMENTS

The authors would like to thank series editors Rich Ling, Gerard Goggin, and Leopoldina Fortunati for their belief in this work and for all the guidance and support that they gave in the development of this project. They would also like to thank Hallie Stebbins, Hannah Doyle, and Jamie Chu at Oxford University Press for their assistance in seeing this project through to publication.

Kathleen would like to thank her research assistant, Ms. Brittany DiFalco, for her assistance in transcription. She would also like to thank all of her participants, who were so willing to share their stories of loss. She gives many thanks to her coauthor, Larissa Hjorth, for her dedication to this project and her diligence in its preparation. This project would not be complete without the love and support of friends, family, and colleagues. Kathleen would like to dedicate this book to her wife, Robin Garber, her mother, Mae Cumiskey, to her mentors, Dr. Michelle Fine and Dr. Lee Jussim, and to those departed souls for whom this book was written.

ACKNOWLEDGMENTS

Larissa would also like to thank her coauthor Kathleen, and to acknowledge the assistance of the Australian Research Council Linkage with Intel, *Locating the Mobile*. Larissa would like to thank her participants, as well as Jung Moon for her research assistant work on the *Sewol* disaster. Larissa would like to dedicate this book to her mother, Noela Hjorth.

GLOSSARY

ADC	after-death communication
AR	augmented reality
IM	instant messaging
MMS	Multimedia Message Service
mobile media	mobile phones and tablets
SNS	social networking sites
STS	science and technology studies
UCC	user-created content

1

Introduction to Mobile Media and Loss

In Cebu, a daughter holds a mobile phone with text messages from her parents lost in Typhoon Haiyan, checking old messages they had sent. She holds the phone as if it contains her parents' spirits. In Washington, DC, a woman carries around her old phone, refusing to get it upgraded because it has a text messaging from her father who has passed away. In Manila, a mother receives text messages from her husband days after he passed away at sea. In Tokyo, friends build an online memorial for a friend lost during the tsunami, floods, and Fukushima disaster of March 2011 (known as 3/11) on the social media platform LINE. In Seoul, a girl posts a memorial to her lost brother on the social media site KakaoStory. In New York, a young woman replays a video on her iPad that she took of her mother before she passed away, so she can feel her presence.

In South Korea, when Soo-hyun's brother was killed in the April 2014 *Sewol* ferry disaster, her mobile phone became a shrine and vessel for channeling her grief and memorializing her brother. The mobile phone—as a device interweaving material and immaterial specters —has become integral in her grieving processes. From the screen saver image of him on her phone, to the ghostly data traces of him left in the form of text messaging and IM (Instant Messaging), to social media pages contained within it, her phone plays an important role on many tacit levels. It helps to channel the complex array of emotions involved through its attunement, which is both intimate and yet public.

So, too, when Maria suddenly lost her brother to a heart attack in the streets of Manila, it was the holding of his phone that gave her comfort in the dark moments of grief. She would scroll through his text messages, his Facebook page, and his e-mails as if retracing the moments before he died to uncover more about the life he led and the emotions he was feeling as his death approached. For many families and friends left behind, the replaying of details obscured through time and the magnifying of particular moments related to the loss of a loved one is a familiar path. Mobile media allow for types of temporal and spatial distances and co-presence to be transgressed—a practice amplified in the case of death. Maria continued to pay her brother's phone bill for six months after his death—as if shutting down the phone would close the last avenue to her brother. For Maria, her brother's phone represented a digital extension of him, a digital ghost left behind to keep her company, as well as a memorial used to reminisce about him and to revisit shared memories.

Digital media increasingly play a key role in the representing, sharing, and remembering of loss. Or, as Dorthe Refslund Christensen and Stine Gotved note, digital media not only redefine death and its processes in terms of "*mediation* (the representation of something through media)" and "*remediation* (the representation of one medium in another)," but also "*mediatization* (the process through which core elements of a social or cultural activity assume media form)" (2015, 1). This process is heightened in the case of mobile media. Mobile media are exemplary of this phenomenon—they provide a continuum between older technologies and practices, while at the same time remediating rituals. Thus, mobile media progressively become embedded within placemaking and memorial culture.

From accessing Facebook tribute pages during public disasters to the lingering digital traces on a smartphone of someone deceased, mobile media are both extending earlier memorial practices, such as photography, and creating new ways in which death and loss manifest within our daily lives (Gibbs et al. 2015b; Brubaker et al. 2012; Graham et al. 2013; Lingel 2013; Church 2013; Deger 2006, 2008; Gibson 2008, 2015; Nansen et al. 2015; Refslund Christensen and Gotved 2015). Mobile media encompass a variety of platforms, techniques, and affordances that allow us to understand processes of continuity and discontinuity, mediation and remediation. Mobile media practices have taught us a lot about the fabric of contemporary life, and they increasingly provide us with ways to understand how death and afterlife are negotiated, ritualized, and reimagined, especially within the everyday.

The ubiquity of digital specters in our everyday lives is particularly apparent in mobile media use, spanning smartphones, iPads, iPhones, and tablets. Mobile media—entangled within the practices of everyday life—provide a visibility around the interweaving textures between the ante- (before), peri- (just around), and post- (after) mortem cultures within quotidian rituals and routines (Gotved 2014). The emotional and affective power of the mobile—as an assemblage of material, symbolic, and immaterial practices—within everyday rituals has been noted by scholars such as Jane Vincent, Leopoldina Fortunati, and Amparo Lasén (Vincent and Fortunati 2009; Vincent 2010; Lasén 2004).

Mobile media entangle various forms of material, social, online, and digital media in specific ways that are both *intimate* and yet *public*. Mobile media practices, such as text messaging, shape, and are shaped by, tacit and official forms of etiquette such as gift-giving (Taylor and Harper 2002), whereby respect, trust, reciprocity, and obligation are all interwoven. These processes of exchange and repository are further complicated when death enters the equation. Mobile media have been analyzed for their power to transgress distinctions between public and private, between intimate and distant, through various modes of co-presence (Ito 2003). And yet the growing role of mobile media to transgress modes of presence, co-presence, and telepresence in contexts of loss and death has been relatively overlooked. Mobile media are vessels for afterlife co-presence at numerous levels—from the memorialization of social media platforms like Facebook pages to storing data specters such as text messaging and camera phone images of the departed to reanimating the dead through mobile media. Co-presence is a useful notion for thinking through the way in which grief, as an unending process that changes and evolves over time, moves in and around mobile media. Mobile media further extend the haunting of someone's data after they pass away. A variety of media practices that encompass social networking (such as Facebook, e-mails, text messaging, and camera phone images), allow for multiple traces of representations and identities to remain beyond physical death.

Haunting Hands considers the various dimensions of mobile media practice within processes of loss—specifically in and around grief, trauma, and bereavement. This is not a manual or a "how to grieve through new media" guide, but rather an exploration into the unique ways in which mobile media recalibrate rituals around death, grieving, and processes of memorialization and provide a sense-making context in ways that are both *intimate* and yet *networked*. Through sense-making processes, we not only engage with rituals about remembering the dead, but also try to integrate the loss into our everyday lives—lives that are both digital and offline. As one of today's most intimate and ubiquitous devices (Fortunati 2002), the mobile phone can provide insight into how we process, represent, and share (or not share) practices and rituals around negotiating grief in an age of accelerated, networked, and emplaced digital data. In sum, mobile media inflect the growing density of digital data in ways that are both *intimate* and yet *public.*

In order to provide a context for *Haunting Hands,* this introduction firstly outlines some of the discussions around the role of memory, mobile media, and culturally specific notions of grief. We then outline some of the key characteristics of mobile media practices that recalibrate particular forms of intimacy through a sense of a networked public that makes intimate the fabric of what it means to be a public, or to be part of a public. We then discuss the methods deployed in the book, and finish with a roadmap of the particular cartographies of mobile media loss we explore. Far from being exhaustive, *Haunting Hands* seeks to provide some nuanced understandings of the complex, dynamic, and rapidly changing role of mobile media in processes of loss as part of a broader context of technological, cultural, social, linguistic, and generational shifts.

MOBILE MEMORIES: MEMORY, MOBILE MEDIA AND CULTURALLY SPECIFIC NOTIONS OF GRIEF

As Connor Graham, Martin Gibbs, and Lanfranco Aceti argue, new media are affording people's lives today to be "extended, prolonged, and ultimately transformed through the new circulations, repetitions, and recontextualizations on the Internet and other platforms" (2013, 133). Digital data allow new ways in which to construct one's life, death, and afterlife (Gotved 2014; Brubaker et al. 2015). With online data affording new pathways for representing and experiencing life, death, and afterlife, much of the literature has focused upon online memorials (de Vries and Rutherford 2004) and other forms of grieving online (Veale 2003).

Graham et al. (2013) argue that with the interweaving of the online and offline lives into the everyday, this digital shadow haunts death and after-death processes, rituals, and representation. Unlike Victorian rituals of death (Walter et al. 2011), which compartmental- ized death to the grave, and traditional psychological models, which construct losses as something that one can "get over" (Rosenblatt 1996), the role of the digital in after-death life means that "death and (after-) death are, once again, becoming more public and every- day" (Graham et al. 2013, 136). This quotidan placement of death is amplified in the rhythms of mobile media within everyday life.

For memory scholar Andrew Hoskin, the rise of mobile media has led to what he calls a "post-scarcity memorial media boom" (2011, 270). Digital materiality expert Margaret Gibson sees these media creating a sense of immediacy in, and around, disasters and trauma— and thus they bring mourning into everyday "with little or no delay (2015, 339)." Mobile media also, Gibson argues, accelerate the cycle of the past haunting in the future through what she calls "a regenera- tive media archive" (2015, 339). As Refslund Christensen and Gotved observe, "media are materialities that allow us to communicate with the dead or about the dead over the gaps between the world of the living and whatever spatial and temporal sphere the dead may reside in without being absorbed into these gaps ourselves" (2015, 1). In this, they are referring to the rise of digital afterlife roles such as "stew- arding" (or managing online media of a posthumous loved one) that involve often invisible and yet symbolic practices not often acknowl- edged in the visual labor of social media (Brubaker 2016).

Increasingly, the mobile phone is not just a companion, wit- ness, repository, and disseminator of events; it also amplifies a type of affect in the way in which events are experienced. As Penelope Papailias notes, using the notion of "viral" better "captures the tem- porality, spatiality, materiality, and mimeticism of these formations, as well as their frequent pathologization" (2016, 1). She argues that the "contemporary performative public mourning follows from mediated witnessing in the era of networked digital media, forming a witnessing/mourning assemblage" (1). The layering of mediated and mediating witness is a complex tapestry when it comes to mobile media. The intimate and immediate "affect" of mobile media means that the witnessing affect is more embodied. For example, the impact of Japan's 3/11 (2011) tragedy upon the world is indistinguishable from the horror-laden mobile phone footage of the wave engulfing cars and houses as if they were toys. This footage had a significant *affect* and *effect* that differed from traditional media depictions of the event. After South Korea's ferry MV *Sewol* sunk on April 16, 2014—a disaster in which over 250 schoolchildren drowned—mobile phone footage of the deceased provided damning evidence of procedures gone wrong. Selfies—some taken by children as young as eight years of age—showed terrifying scenes of people panicking. These selfies-as-eulogies demonstrated emergent ways in which mobile media practices were recalibrating the relationship between peri- and postmortem modes of representation and witnessing. Here the camera phone footage was not just evidence for court prosecutors and for the grieving families of the deceased; the trauma-laden images also became highly affective memorials that spread quickly and worked to consolidate a worldwide public outcry.

These are but two of the multiple ways in which the ubiquity of mobile phones is transforming how we experience, share, and represent events of emotional significance in our lives during disasters. In particular, they highlight the diverse registers of "memory capital" (Reading 2009) as linked to national citizenship and transnational human value chains. Here we can think of Pierre Bourdieu's (1979) work on "capital" as a form of knowledge. In both the 3/11 and Sewol examples, we see the way mobile media is used to construct types of memory knowing and knowledges that afford specific forms of intimacy within a networked public. Mobile media both continue and remediate older forms of memory practices such as photography, letter writing, and rituals of representation. While we acknowledge the important work conducted in memory studies around digital media (Hoskins 2011; Volkmer 2006; Richardson and Hessey 2009; Ernst 2012; Hand 2013; van Dijck 2007), in *Haunting Hands* we focus squarely upon mobile media (Reading 2009a, 2009b), which we argue shape, and are shaped by, memory practices that differ from other media contexts.

Specifically, mobile media play a key role in the *context* and *content* of representation, dissemination, and affect that require a specific lens to understand the "witnessing" phenomenon. Mobile media involve many platforms and affordances that allow us to consider the role of media *beyond* a platform. For example, much of the work around online memorialization has viewed Facebook as a default setting for social media and social networking. And yet there are many countries where Facebook is not synonymous with social media. Moreover, many social media users deploy what Madianou and Miller (2012) would call "polymedia" that compartmentalize different types of intimacies and publics. The intimate affordance of mobile media as an extension of the body and an always-on device means that those intimate public tapestries take particular forms. The affordances of mobile media are heightened in, and around, the practices and rituals associated with loss. While media broadcasting of responses to disasters and trauma is an important area of scholarship related to this study, *Haunting Hands* centers upon the intimate, personal stories around mobile media and loss.

Intimacy has always been mediated—if not by technologies, then by memory, language, and gestures—and intimacy is also culturally specific. In this book, we focus upon understanding the role that cultural context plays in defining the multiple and specific ways in which grief and loss can be understood, experienced, and represented via mobile media. In this analysis, we draw from primary and secondary data to consider the layering and textures of representation and meaning-making around intimate understandings of loss in and through mobile media.

Different methods are used to reflect the nuances of each context. For example, in the discussion of selfies in the Sewol disaster, we focus predominantly on secondary data on YouTube and social media. We sourced media in both English and Hangul to gauge a sense of the enormity of the event and its impact upon the emotional fabric of the public. We also wanted to be careful about respecting the families of the deceased and their mourning processes, and we have therefore intentionally obscured the identities of many of the deceased, unless they had become public figures representative of the disaster. This material is contrasted with the empirical work of the spoken word artist Klare Lanson, in which her public work around mourning and digital traces means that we identify her but not her interviewees. In the United States and Australian interviews, the confidentiality of the participants is preserved through pseudonyms.

Drawing upon a social-constructionist perspective that focuses on cultural differences in grief (Rosenblatt 2000) and the notion that grief is not something that ends (Rosenblatt 1996), this book explores the ways in which mobile media are entangled with changing practices, understandings, rituals, and etiquettes around grief and loss. As Robert A. Neimeyer, Dennis Klass, and Michael Robert Dennis note, the construction of dominant Western psychological conceptions of bereavement as a largely intrapsychic process is misguided. Rather, grief is a social and cultural process whereby meanings are "found, appropriated, or assembled" between people as much as within them (2014, 485). As they observe,

> Far from being a private and dispassionate cognitive process, contending with the meaning of the loss and the meaning of our lives in the wake of it, is typically deeply emotional, intricately

social, and inevitably constructed and sometimes contested in broader linguistic and cultural contexts. That is, although grief and mourning may be universal and biological, both the story of the death itself and our changed relationship to the deceased are personally narrated, socially shared, and expressed in compliance with or contradiction to widely varying communal rules. (486)

Grief, like mobile media, is inherently informed by the social and by widely varying communal rules. It is as inextricably interwoven within the social as it is within the cultural. It is indicative of intimate publics. The experience of mourning, while at times a private experience, is one that is unique to the individual, and as such it becomes an experience that is constituted through reflection, individualized through the interpretations of events, and understood in conversation with others. Mobile media, as emotionally investigated and intimately charged devices, can provide us with insight into contemporary moral and cultural economies and values that are being shaped by, and are shaping, changing processes in how we communicate, share, memorialize, and understand loss.

Moreover, as mundane devices, mobile media afford pathways into multiple online and offline entanglements across text messaging, various applications, digital archives, camera phones, IM, and social media, through which users engage emotional ties to others—ties that take on ghostly features after a death or loss occurs. A multidimensional view of bereavement allows for a mobile device to become a mechanism for the processing of grief. These affordances, however, do not at once encourage the integration of mobile devices into funereal traditions (Nansen et al. 2015; Haverinen 2014). Mobile media may confound the transitions between the necessary private moments of grief and those more easily shared.

Examining mobile-mediated linking objects and digital forms of memorialization can highlight the ways mobile media imbricate processes of identity and sociality. Through its assemblage of intimate yet public textures, mobile media make us reconsider the relationship between death and afterlife, especially with the digital afterlife and posthumous performativity still relatively underexplored (Stanyek and Piekut 2010). In the next section, we discuss this lingering in terms of reconceptualizing death and afterlife.

RECONSTRUCTIONS OF DEATH AND AFTERLIFE

Death has enduringly offered anthropologists a unique theoretical conundrum in that it concerns humans and human personhood and yet unlike most aspects of social life, it involves an absent interlocutor. A terrifying rupture into mundane existence, death demands a response on the part of individuals and communities. . . . The destruction of human life at once redefines personhood through its destruction or reorientation, forces metaphysical contemplation in ways that typically open a window onto the sacred, and reproduces the social order through a loss that challenges its integrity. (Straight 2010, 127–28)

Bilinda Straight (2010) identifies anthropological approaches to grief and death as both erupting from and transcending social life. Identifying the legacy of Robert Hertz's (1960) observation of death as involving three "actors"—the soul, the corpse, and the mourners—Straight notes the Eurocentric focus of such an approach. Moreover, in an age of online and mobile media, the mobile media device unquestionably becomes another actor in, and around, the grieving process. Straight also draws on Marilyn Strathern's (1988) discussion of dividual and individual subjectivity as a useful dichotomy in which to move beyond Eurocentric approaches.

For Strathern, as opposed to the Eurocentric "individual," the "dividual" subject is plural, "containing a generalized sociality within" (1988, 13). Straight comprehensively addresses the multiple dichotomies associated with death (e.g., mortality versus immortality; material versus spiritual, body versus soul) noting that the way to undermine such binaries is by examining the cultural and temporal contexts. As graves move from just being geographically situated in cemeteries to taking multiple and fragmented presences online and within devices, grief and mourning become ubiquitously located in the everyday and mundane (Graham et al. 2013). As Straight notes, "memory management" (Lohmann 2007) can take various forms of memorialization. She observes the following:

> Whether memorialization practices preserve or destroy mementos of the deceased turns on mourners' unique relationships to lost persons. These relationships can change over time as living persons' grief softens or memories of the deceased transform. In very painful cases, memory must be controlled by destruction of objects associated with deceased persons while in other cases objects are preserved and cherished. . . . However, no matter how the work of memory and the imagination is performed, it is the living who remember, and they do so by continuing a social relationship in some form. (2010, 138)

In addition, the co-presence afforded by mobile media offers not only the extension of remembering to take place in the mundane everyday, but also for it to extend beyond the lifetime of those doing the remembering. So what do digital artifacts offer in the way of memorialization that differ from their pre-digital counterparts? Take, for example, photography and the recent case of Vivian Maier. While Maier worked in various guises such as a nanny, her real calling and passion was photography. A natural at composition, her photos became a lens for a changing world. After her death, Maier's photos were discovered, and she became a world-renowned artist overnight thanks, in part, to the role of digital media. According to curator Louise Neri, Maier's work represented an analog epoch: "If she had been born into our time, perhaps she would be a more socialized person. She would have Facebook friends. She might have a huge following, in fact. It's a real then-and-now story" (cited in Bunbury 2014).

However, part of Maier's posthumous success was the ability of her work to be disseminated and shared. Maier's life as a nanny seemed one in which she enjoyed being alone and observing, and thus we may consider her to be the type of person not likely to embrace social media or selfies. Here it is important to remember that death and grief online need to be contextualized within particular cultural and historical milieus. The ability for anyone to digitize our lives after our death highlights our inability to control our digital legacies and the ways in which we have the potential to live on in the creative imaginations of others. User-created digital resurrections can happen spontaneously and without our needed permission or the permission of our loved ones.

As Neimeyer, Prigerson, and Davies argue, "the meaning-making triggered by loss is pursued at the juncture of self and system rather than only in the private thoughts and feelings of the bereaved individual. Thus, the self is constituted and reconstituted in relation to an embracing social world" (2002, 239). In Pamela Roberts's (2004) article on "virtual cemeteries," she defines three outcomes of online bereavement communities: to continue bonds (with the dead), to strengthen relationships (with the living), and to create new online communities. Mobile media also force us to embrace the hybridization of liveness and deadness. The term *liveness* emphasizes the immediacy of experiences over the state of being "alive." As a concept, it has attracted much critique as part of the rhetoric and performance of new media (Auslander 1999). Liveness has a particular currency within mobile media practices (Baker 2013; Farman 2011). The rise of mobile media within UCC citizen journalism, and other forms of live broadcasting has been described as part of an intimate turn in which audiences want seemingly unmediated quotidian experiences (Meikle 2011). Liveness debates have underscored debates around the so-called newness of new media in the form of remediation—as we will discuss below (Bolter and Grusin 1999). Online memorials both remediate and reinvent pathways and modes of grieving in changing intimate public contexts. It is within these changing intimate public contexts that reconstructions of life, death, and the afterlife take place.

In addition, social expectations and cultural norms may not readily be adapted to include these augmented ways of mourning. We attempt to allow for resistance to using technology this way throughout the book. This resistance does not take the form of not using technology. Instead, it emerges in the ways in which mobile media use is always being negotiated as both a continuum for older rituals and a space for emergent practices. Take, for example, the emergent role of "stewarding" social media accounts of the deceased. Stewarding is the process whereby digital data of the dead is curated and organized by loved ones. Stewarding is usually taken up by loved ones during the grieving process—for some, a far from ideal time due to the negotiation of loss and stress. Furthermore, there are no rulebooks and the etiquette is often tacit (Brubaker 2016). This is but one of the many emerging phenomena whereby we have yet to comprehend the ways in which deceased digital data can live on. Understanding these dynamic processes means we need to provide a context for mobile media and grief that is both intimate and public.

INTIMATE PUBLICS AND PUBLIC INTIMACY

Mobile media amplify inner subjectivities as they conform to particular sociocultural rituals and practices (Pertierra 2006). Because of their ubiquitous, intimate, and personalized nature (Fortunati 2002; Lasén 2004), mobile media devices are also increasingly vessels for intimate publics and mobile intimacy. Mobile intimacy overlays the electronic with the social, the emotional with co-presence, and allows the device itself to be transformed into a portable memory box. With the rise of mobile social media, different forms of individual and public participation can be intertwined with ways of communicating that are personalized, embodied, and emplaced, and that can generate a sense of intimacy and closeness.

Smartphone users often integrate their mobile media use into their daily experiences and rhythms. This integration creates an expansion of the domains of social interaction, as well as an expansion in the ways in which experiences will be remembered and shared. Mobile media make intimate the notion of public through the personalized, mobile-mediated sharing of localized experiences (e.g., personal pictures posted on Facebook of a trip to the Empire State Building in New York City); and make public the notion of intimacy (e.g., sharing via Twitter the pain of a recent heartbreak, while on public transportation) (Hjorth and Arnold 2013). The ongoing narration of activities through text messaging and social media, live broadcasts, and group messaging via the mobile device establishes a sense of connection to remote others that is ceaseless. Remote others impact and affect one's current context by making their presence known through text messaging or social media updates, or in remnants of their influence stored in past text messages, voicemails, digital photos, or notes. These practices create both seamless and seamful moments in the rhythms of everyday life, in that at times we may effortlessly engage with mobile media as a part of our experiences and at other times the mobile device may interrupt, distract, and disrupt.

This kind of engagement with mobile media is occurring simultaneously in an online world generated by the very same technologies and applications that are inherently social and often public. That is, the forms of intimacy engendered through social media platforms are often played out, and indeed performed, in a public online domain. The idea that forms of intimacy might be generated in contexts that are at the same time public is not new. Lauren Berlant observed, in an article published before social media had become an integral part of everyday worlds, that intimacy has taken on new geographies and forms of mobility, most notably as a kind of "publicness" (1998, 281).

However, in a digital material environment, intimate relations are not simply performed in pairs or bounded groups; rather, they traverse the online and offline. They are performed in physically public worlds but in electronic privacy (such as when someone privately sends a friend a camera phone image of herself in a café), and in an electronic public that is geographically private (such as when we read personal messages posted to us on a Facebook page or on Twitter, while in the private space of our homes). As Mimi Sheller argues, "there are new modes of public-in-private and private-in-public that disrupt commonly held spatial models of these as two separate 'spheres'" (2014, 39).

Advancing this concept further, Hjorth and Arnold (2013) have proposed a concept of intimate publics, through which we can understand the competing histories, identities, and practices within the Asia-Pacific region. They suggest that we should understand that such intimate publics are increasingly being shaped by new forms of "mobile intimacy" (Hjorth and Lim 2012); that is, by the ways in which intimacy and our various forms of mobility (across technological, geographic, psychological, physical, and temporal differences) infuse public and private spaces through mobile media's simultaneous mediation of both intimacy and space. These new forms of mobile intimacy, therefore, underpin some of the ways in which life and death are represented—or, as Graham et al. note, "how publics are formed and connected with through different technologies as much as which publics are created and networked" (2013, 135). Since the devices are carried by the user, these spaces of mobile intimacy and intimate spaces made mobile become, on some level, embodied by the user. Embodiment in the digital age is then produced through the entanglement of the virtual and the material (Farman 2011). And in this, a further mobile intimacy may develop solely as that between user and device.

METHODS

In this book, we draw on a social-constructivist approach across various disciplines such as media, cultural studies, anthropology, and psychology. The book represents ongoing research into the role of mobile media in memorialization and grieving processes. Through the lens of mobile media, we hope to chart how the ways we grieve are changing, as well as understanding the continuities within older ritualization processes. Through mobile media we can develop new ways of understanding cultural rituals related to life and death that are more than simplistic dichotomies between mortality and immortality. Just as the online is an embedded part of the social and routine, we explore processes of grief and loss as part of a similar entanglement. We deploy textual and ethnographic techniques and analysis to the field and utilize cross-cultural case studies to consider how grief is inextricably bound to its specific social and cultural context.

Through the adoption of a social-constructivist approach, this book discusses various examples of grief from a variety of cultural, generational, and ideological contexts. While some of our examples are drawn from public forms of grief, such as the Korean ferry disaster, others explore individual loss and how mobile media can connect us to both traditional and new grieving rituals and processes, as well as change how we relate to life, death, and the concept of the afterlife. We conducted interviews in Korea, Australia, Japan, and the United States. Pseudonyms are used for all participants except for the performance artist Klare Lanson, who used mobile media to channel the collective trauma of natural disaster on her community into stories of hope and resilience (see Chapter 3).

In total, we have collected over one hundred interviews in a variety of locations to allow us to explore the culturally specific dimensions of loss and mobile media use. Interviews with Korean, Australian, and Japanese participants involved discussions in and around scenarios of use that included talking about emotions around mobile and social media. In these interviews, screen shots of key visuals were taken and de-identified through obscuring names and faces. The interviews were participant-led, so that participants felt in control of the information they disclosed without becoming distressed. Some of the interviews were conducted via e-mail, while others were conducted face-to-face. Participants chose what method best suited them. Interviews conducted in the United States were all done face-to-face using a semi-structured interviewing style.

Loss was broadly defined for the participants, especially those in the United States, and while the majority of participants had experienced the death of a loved one, other participants came to talk about other losses such as relationship breakups, the loss of a home, the loss of a pet, and so on. Bringing together the often disparate discussions in psychology, media, and cultural studies around media and loss, *Haunting Hands* provides an interdisciplinary probing into how mobile media facilitates particular modes of grieving, affect, and loss. We consider the cultural dimensions of emotion and some of the debates on psychological models (Ahmed 2004) by connecting to historical and cross-cultural models for grieving. For example, the queer cultural theorist Sara Ahmed argues for an understanding of the "cultural politics of emotion" (2004), whereby she de-naturalizes many of the Western binaries around emotion. The chosen title of this book, *Haunting Hands,* recognizes the fact that mobile-emotive practices only take place when they are in the hands of the user. As we will demonstrate, the effects of this enactment can be quite haunting, but only if the user experiences their device as a site through which they can cultivate and conjure connections to their loss and to the mourning process.

STRUCTURE OF THE BOOK

This book is divided into two sections. The first section explores "mobile-emotive" grief rituals. By "mobile-emotive" we mean the adaptation of culturally specific, affect-laden rituals in and around mobile media practices. The particular rituals we highlight focus on grief responses. The second section, titled "Ghosts in the Mobile," explores the ways in which the mobile device can become haunted, digitally and materially, and contribute to the building of an *occulture* not readily recognized or acknowledged. In this introduction (Chapter 1) we outline some of the key contexts to this book as well as methods and structure. In Chapter 2 we outline some of the book's key concepts (using data from US interviews) such as mobile-emotive co-presence and reconstructions of death and afterlife through the lens of mobile media.

Chapter 3 begins the first section of the book, where we explore how the mobile-emotive co-presence of mobile media can be experienced as a form of companionship and through remediated rituals of death and afterlife. Drawing on fieldwork done predominantly in Australia, Chapter 3 considers how the mobile phone can facilitate a kind of constant companionship that can be a lifesaver in times of extreme emotional suffering, and can assist users in both practical and affective aspects of the grieving process. We look at a sound poet who has used mobile media and the digital cloud as a way to explore the trauma of being involved in the Victorian (Australia) floods of 2011, in which her house and all her possessions were destroyed.

In Chapters 4 and 5, we begin to integrate mobile media into contemporary theory and practices around grief and mourning. These chapters are based on the interviews conducted with participants in the United States. In Chapter 4, we discuss the private nature of mobile media and how it can focus on mobile-emotive rituals of affirmation and intensification as it relates to social identity. Loss can be viewed as a disruption in one's personal and social identity. Mobile media are used in rituals of affirmation and intensification as a means to better understand the role that the deceased played in the bereaved person's life. Mobile media are also used to intensify connections between people who share a common identity. This chapter demonstrates the ways in which users utilize social and mobile media to express collective social identities and acknowledge the significance of others. The role of affect in mobile-emotive expressions of grief, and the ways in which loss can change users' relationships with technology, is also discussed in this chapter.

Chapter 5 focuses on transition and letting go. Traditional Western psychological trajectories of the grief process typically end with the concept of "letting go" of the deceased or "lost object." While this book engages with critiques related to this trajectory, this chapter focuses on the ways in which the concept of letting go functions in terms of users' relationships with digital content. Drawing from the US interviews, this chapter will show the role that the purging—as well as preserving—of mobile media plays in the integration of loss into one's life and that mobile media practices can also demonstrate changes or transitions in the grieving process.

In Chapter 6, the start of the second section of the book, we explore the interconnection of mobile media and loss in the *Sewol* ferry disaster of 2014. This specific disaster was one in which mobile media featured prominently, especially in terms of lingering incriminations from the mobile phones of the 250 drowned school children. In South Korea, mobile media have played a key role—literally and symbolically—in the nation's soft (economic) power growth. The significance of mobile media politically, socially, and culturally highlights the specific affordances of mobile media as intimate publics. In particular, studying this disaster allows us to understand how the selfie can operate as a eulogy for those who are deceased, as well as a powerful vehicle for mobilizing a public. Here the selfie-as-eulogy operates to create a haunting and mobilization through its affective witnessing processes—in how it mobilizes emotions, memories, and publics.

Chapter 7 begins with a quasi-historical overview of dominant mortuary practices and rituals from a Western perspective. This overview seeks to connect new media with and provide some context on the ways in which these older practices relate to their media genealogies. The focus is on the open nature of mobile communication and the ways in which this then lends itself to be the perfect medium, like a psychomanteum, through which parapsychological phenomena can be experienced. In this chapter we return to the interviews conducted in the United States and explore the ways in which mobile media can facilitate a continuation of bonds, in typical and atypical ways, with the deceased beyond death. This mobile-emotive form of after-death communication provides a means through which we can begin to conceptualize a new sense of immortality and reimagine the meaning of death.

Chapter 8 is our concluding chapter. In it we reflect on the field and explore some propositions for future research in this area. From selfies at funerals and the issues of digital ghosts in an age of "big data," to how mobile media is increasingly playing a key role in the representation and affect of public tragedy and mourning, this chapter seeks to explore some of the speculative issues for future research.

Haunting Hands seeks to bring together a variety of mobile media experiences in and around the grief process. As mentioned previously, this is not a guide, but rather an exploration of changing rituals and modes of memorialization. It is not meant to be exhaustive, but instead seeks to be a nuanced study of some of the ways in which this phenomenon is playing out. The book seeks to initiate the conversation around how can we further understand the politics and ethics of dealing with the mobile data traces left by those departed. We begin the conversation by exploring what it means to be intimate with mobile data of the dead. And while older generations still often live their lives predominantly offline, future questions will need to consider how we account for the dense overload of data that will continue to haunt us after the user has passed away. One thing is certain, just as mobile media practices and deployment have been uneven, so too will the differences be amplified through various cultural and religious contexts as we increasingly deal with data hauntings of those alive and dead.

2

Co-present Reconstructions of Death, Loss, and Mourning

My sister posted the picture of the funeral on Instagram. At first I was like, "why would you do it so soon?" But I could understand her reasoning. Because of the people that didn't make it that were close family, that were so intimate but that couldn't make it because it was so last minute. [And] people *liked* [the photo], and then I was confused about that too, because how could you like a picture of a dead woman? And then I understood why they liked it and commented on it because they were saying stuff like, "Oh your mom, even to this day, is beautiful." I was like, "Thanks, thanks for putting that up." (Laila, 18, Hispanic/Latina, US)

At first, Laila's private and intimate moment surrounding the death of her mother was shared with only her immediate family, who were physically present at the funeral. That moment was rendered public when her sister decided to share photos of her mother in the casket on social media. This sharing became a way of including in the experience other close family members who were not able to attend the funeral—to create an experience of mobile-emotive co-presence to transgress the temporal, spatial, and geographic boundaries of the funeral. However, the intimate and yet public nature of mobile-emotive co-presence can create various textures in the grieving experience, since it can create multiple hermeneutic responses. Through the public sharing of the photo, the intimacy of the funeral was transformed by the public and broadcast nature of social media (Gibson 2015).

As Laila's experience demonstrates, through mobile media, events are not only accelerated in their dissemination, but they also come with complex and multiple potential intimacies and associated interpretations. The rapid adoption of mobile devices around the world makes their presence in any and all contexts—including the moment of death and at a funeral—no longer an anomaly. Users often rely on their own devices to document or render significant what is taking place around them. As Brooke Wendt notes regarding selfies, they are used to create a sense of recognition (2014). Even with the global and local disparities that exist in access to mobile media, growing numbers of people around the world are utilizing their mobile devices to extend their storehouse of emotional experiences beyond the immediate (Vincent and Fortunati 2009). These experiences can then be shared with remote others instantaneously.

Through the sharing of emotional content via social media or group messaging, users are generating a kind of shared consciousness where others can join in, comment, and influence how individuals process their grief experiences and the mourning process (Petierra 2013). This kind of shared consciousness also allows users to, at times, *not* share content, and instead store deeply meaningful and emotional content on their devices for their own private and personal uses. Such images are now readily accessible to them at a moment's notice, creating an additional realm of intimacy rarely shared. Mobile media can be understood as generating a sense of intimacy in users. This sense of intimacy is extended into significant experiences via the persons with whom the device connects. In the context of traumatic events, the smartphone as camera phone can be a witness, a companion, and an alibi (via photographic evidence) to the unfolding events. As noted in Chapter 1, the multiple platforms within mobile media allow for different modes of intimacy and public sharing simultaneously.

The archiving of meaningful events on mobile devices intensifies the sense of attachment to one's device, which then makes attachment (to both the device and to others) the central building block in the creation of environments of co-presence. Mira (18, Egyptian/Turkish, US) indicated that she was comfortable in sharing her laptop with her family, but when asked about her comfort level with sharing her iPhone she responded:

> No I would not! That's my privacy! People don't like their phones being touched. It's not like I'm hiding anything secret, it's just like a part of me in that I always have it. I'll go to the bathroom with it, take a shower with it. It's like a part of you. It's always with me, next to me. I go to school with it. Whenever it is raining, cold, windy, snowing, it is always there. So I feel like it's kind of like a human being. It gets everything. At the same time, it is how I contact [and] communicate with people. And even though I lost my friends and stuff, this has been helping me do something else: think about other things. It helps me get away from whatever is bothering me.

In this passage, in the US context, the mobile phone is described as an extension of self and something attached to the user, as well as something the user is emotionally attached to. This description extends the meaning of the personal, portable, and pedestrian nature of the device (Ito, Okabe, and Matsuda 2005) to include an emotional and psychological dimension (Vincent 2010). Mira went so far as to compare her device to a human being—and in her case, after losing ties with most of her peer group over an argument, her mobile phone became her sole companion and a portal of escape as well as connection. The intimate co-presence she felt she had with the device resulted from the ease with which she could access meaningful *content* stored on it, as well as the *contact* that she could make via her device. These intimate connections *with* the mobile and *via* the mobile seems to allow some users to be able to share emotionally laden content with others more easily through their devices than they might do face-to-face.

Mira's relationship to her mobile phone is indicative of its significance as a form of mobile-emotive co-presence. The term *co-presence* was first popularized by Erving Goffman in his seminal work, *The Presentation of Self in Everyday Life* (1956). The term then became adopted by the Internet and mobile communication fields to represent the mediated experience of feelings in the presence of remote others. Co-presence emphasizes the device's ability to assist the user in formulating an intensely emotional and affective augmented reality that is ever-present but not dependent on a stable relationship with physical structures (outside of the necessary infrastructure for mobile communication—the device itself, cell towers, power sources, satellites, etc.). Mobile-emotive contexts provide the "space" for intimate co-presence, whereby presence is about *psychological* rather than *physical* proximity.

Literature around co-presence within mobile communication fields flourished with the work of Christian Licoppe (2004) and Mizuko Ito (2003) as a productive way of rethinking traditional binaries that are no longer adequate for everyday life. Broadly defined, co-presence can be understood as "the degree to which geographically dispersed agents experience a sense of physical and/or psychological proximity through the use of particular communication technologies" (Milne 2010, 165). The concept of co-presence deliberately conceives of presence as a spectrum of engagement across multiple pathways of connection—and thus goes beyond counterproductive dichotomous models of online and offline, here and there, virtual and actual, the physical and the immaterial (Sconce 2000; Hjorth 2005). The rubric of co-presence provides a broader context for understanding intimacy and mediation as something that is not only a late twentieth- or twenty-first-century phenomenon, but as something that has always been an integral part of being social and being human. The concept also allows us to connect the contemporary with the historical in terms of the evolution of mediated intimacies.

Co-presence can take various forms—spatial, social, temporal, and psychological, to name a few. Co-presence is about multiple forms of connection and haunting that move in and out of now and then, here and there, life and afterlife. The ability to produce emotionally charged, vivid digital content amplifies the experience of mobile-emotive co-presence. The term *mobile-emotive* will be used throughout this book as a term that extends co-presence and Vincent and Fortunati's (2009) term *electronic emotions*. The mobile-emotive includes the ways in which each user may uniquely enact co-presence and other forms of engagement with mobile media to assist in the processing and regulation of the emotional experiences of everyday life—especially those surrounding death and mourning.

The mobile-emotive is *affective* in that affect "represents our emotional investment in our world and each other and the way such investment shapes us" (Valentine 2013, 385). Emotional work deepens "our fundamental dependency on each other and, therefore, our vulnerability" (2013, 385). Mobile-emotive contexts emerge when the mobile device is used to enhance (and at times publicize) emotional aspects of personal situations and unexpected occurrences. Mobile-emotive practices represent the ways in which people cultivate their attachment to the ever-presence of their devices to then include these devices in all aspects of how they perceive and process personal and interpersonal interactions. Jane Vincent describes it this way:

> The mobile phone appears to be much more than a device that
> enables constant and immediate connectivity. Indeed this desire

to not be switched off, not to lose the connection has created the notion of a "dependent presence". . . . The dependent presence occurs as a result of needing and wanting to feel together, to share emotion (electronically), and the ability to be always touching or feeling the mobile phone sates this for some. (2010, 160)

In this chapter we detail examples of mobile-emotive co-presence practices and some of the multiple ways in which reconstructions of death and afterlife are reframed through the lens of mobile media.

DEFINING MOBILE-EMOTIVE PRACTICES

When something happens suddenly and, at times, unexpectedly, mobile media users often turn to their devices for comfort, for acknowledgment, and for a sense of grounding (Vincent and Fortunati 2009). US participant Portia (18, African-American) could not believe that her mother's friend Lucy—who was like a second mom to her—passed away. Despite her mother telling her the news (face-to-face), Portia went on to Facebook for confirmation. Seeing that other people had posted Lucy's picture with condolence messages attached helped make the loss a reality, but the social media posts were not enough. Portia reflected on this:

> I was sleeping. She died like 12 o'clock or 1 o'clock in the morning . . . I was sleeping and my mom whispered in my ear and told me that Lucy died and I am sleeping and I am like "OK, Lucy died." And then I woke up the next day and it really hit me, I called my mom and I said, "I had a dream that Lucy died," and she was like, "Portia, she did die!" I was like "Oh . . ." Everyone was crying. I went on Facebook and saw her. Everyone put up pictures and said "Loving memory" and that day, I didn't cry,

I didn't feel anything until late at night, and then it really hit me. And I just started bawling. I thought that it wasn't real. I wasn't convinced. I had to look and I had to see pictures of her and I was like, "Damn, she really did die" and then I had to call a couple of people and ask: "Did Lucy really die?" and everybody is like, "Yeah she did die." . . . So when I saw that picture [on Facebook], that's when it hit me like, "Wow." She had on a black dress with her smiling. And I saw another picture that I took of her on Mother's Day and that is when it hit me, when I looked at it [on my phone].

Portia turned to social mobile media in her grief. The shared social media moments—alongside pictures and messages stored on her phone and calls to her friends—helped her come to terms with the loss. This is the mobile-emotive tapestry that connects the textures of grief and associated feelings of shock and sadness. Portia then returned to Facebook to look at more pictures, which then motivated her to scroll through the photos she had stored on her phone. Portia did this as a means of grounding herself in the loss. While some participants in our fieldwork clung to their stored content, others wanted to use their mobile devices to escape the reality of the loss and to generate some psychological distance between themselves and the emotionality of the event.

Psychological distance is a fundamental concept within the field of Western psychology. Studies have shown that emotional intensity diminishes with psychological distance (Van Boven et al. 2010). When people experience something as emotionally intense, they perceive a sense of closeness to the experience. The vividness and poignancy of user-created digital content makes it likely that such content—often mobile-mediated—related to loss will be experienced as emotionally intense and psychologically close—the definition of mobile-emotive co-presence. The immediacy of and accessibility to others can serve a multitude of purposes during a crisis (Dutton and Nainoa 2002). The mobile-emotive aspects of engaging with mobile media becomes evident in the ways in which people use their mobile devices as a means to regulate and contain, as well as amplify and intensify, their emotions.

US participants openly discussed the role that mobile media played in mediating emotions related to profound grief, loss, and mourning. While some participants used their devices and apps to deepen their emotional response, others used their devices as a buffer between themselves and their own emotional response. In addition, the devices often became a mediator between themselves and other people's responses. Many participants talked about how strategic they were in deciding whether to text or call or meet face-to-face as it related to how they would share information and their feelings about their losses. These decisions were based mainly on what they thought they could handle emotionally. When asked about how she shared the news about the death of her grandmother, Olivia (19, American, with diverse ethnic background, US) replied,

> Phone calls, Internet, and texting. I know that sounds terrible [that she texted the news], but I don't really like to talk on the phone, not to mention [that] I was in such shock and hysterical crying that I didn't want to talk to anybody on the phone. I called, at the time, my best friend; I was hysterical crying.

Olivia described how she relied on more mediated forms of communication to protect her from having the vulnerability of her mourning revealed to everyone. She mentioned how she does not typically like to talk on the phone, so while experiencing the pain of her grief, she certainly did not want to talk to anybody on the phone, other than her best friend. This discrepancy in use highlights the fact that mobile phone users in the United States made choices about whom they talked to, and those choices were often reflective of the degree of closeness they felt with their conversational partners. In addition, the use of text messaging served as a means of protecting oneself from the emotional impact of receiving and sending messages related to loss. US participant Annie's boyfriend broke up with her via text messaging. His motivation for doing that appeared to be his desire to distance himself from the emotionality of the event. Annie (18, White, US) provided her analysis of the situation:

> When he did it over text message I just felt very like, [he] didn't care about [me] any more, [he] just put down words. But he told me, "I can't look you in the face and do it. I don't want to physically see you hurt. I wouldn't physically hurt you, it just hurts to look at you . . . crying because I've always known you as a happy person so to see you upset hurts me." It was a very easy way out for him I feel.

Annie interpreted her boyfriend's decision to break up with her via text messaging as being cowardly. According to Annie, based on text messages he had sent her, he believed that it would be too emotional for him to break up with her face-to-face. Through text messages, he could break up with her and maintain a certain degree of psychological distance from his deed. Sometimes this psychological distance can be helpful in completing tasks, and mediated communication supports the functionality of those dealing with the psychological impact of loss and the necessary tasks related to grief. During the trauma of breaking up with her boyfriend, Jackie (22, American of Italian and Greek descent, US) noted that text messages were the preferred mode of communication:

> Because you have a lot of time to think about what you are going to write. Things that you want to say, it [may be] embarrassing

[to say] face-to-face. Or you don't know what their reaction is going to be, or you don't know if you are going to wind up crying and not saying anything. That's why I did it through text messaging because I knew if I was going to see him, I was just going to cry. I had to say what I needed to say, and that's why I did it through text message.

In addition to using text messages to communicate emotional content, Jackie, in particular, was adept at describing how important it was for her to create a private space via her device, a space that was separate from the rest of her life where she could reminisce, ruminate, and eventually reconcile her feelings about her romantic breakup. Her well-maintained mobile archive of her whole relationship served as a vehicle through which she could escape the pain. She recalled how she would go through her old text messages every night in an effort to find some peace. This nightly ritual was done alone and was kept secret from others. Jackie believed that this enabled her to be able to pretend (during the day) that the breakup did not impact her emotionally, and she could act as though she were moving on.

One could hear throughout William's (18, Black, US) interview some reluctance to deal directly with material that connected him to the psychological impact and the ultimate reality of the loss he experienced. When we discussed whether or not he had photos of his deceased friend Samuel on his phone, he responded that he wished he had them. He regretted not having any, and he remarked that if he did he would visit them, but not often, because they would trigger painful emotions and memories. In addition, William remarked that he often used his phone as a means of escaping reality. Listening to music, for example, was a means to distract him from the sadness of his friend's passing. He said that listening to music "keeps me level-headed in a way. So it's comfort to me basically."

William's response was similar to other men's responses in the US study. American men in this study were likely to use texting and social media as a means to escape, to control their emotions, and to put troubling thoughts and emotions out of their heads. Elliot (19, White, US) was asked whether texting was more effective for dealing with interpersonal conflicts than voice calls. He responded this way:

> [Texting is] the same probably, except you don't have—you get the same words out but it might be more permanent on a phone because [the text message] is more physical, you can visually see it. I don't know. I feel like it is the same reaction. [If things gets heated over a text message] I'll probably ignore them for like an hour or so, and let it cool off, and then go back like nothing happened. It might be because I am a guy, but I don't know.

Elliot thought his ability to handle arguments over text messages in the same way that he would through voice calls was part of being "a guy." This alludes to the fact that in the US context, men are often expected not to display or show emotion. This expectation could carry over into how these men use social and mobile media. For US participant Nasir (18, Pakistani), his text messaging and social media interaction related to the loss of his grandfather was minimal. He was extremely upset personally, but he was not compelled to reach out to others publicly for support via his mobile device. His quick fix was to put the death out of his head. For Nasir, the goal was to let it go:

> I wasn't really texting. I wasn't really telling anyone about it. I was too upset to do anything. [On Facebook] I just put like, "Rest in Peace." I just put it up because I wanted to get it out of my head. I just want to get stuff out of my head, so I just put a status up there. I really don't express myself too much; I just keep it with

me. I'll express it, but not like crazy. I really don't take anything
to the head.

Nasir's desire to not "take anything to the head" could be his motivation for attempting to resume his normal activities, both on social
media and in his life in general, after the death of his grandfather. As
mentioned previously, not all participants took to social or mobile
media as a means of expressing their emotions or processing their
grief. Many people turned to social media and to their mobile devices
as a means of distraction and escape from the emotional experiences
that they were having. Turning to social media in these contexts was
not done in an effort to garner support or to connect with their loss.
The bereaved may attempt to resume their typical activities via social
and mobile media as a means of escape from the intensity of traumatic events, and as a way to broadcast to others that they are fine
and that they desire to return to a sense of "normalcy." US participant
Nancy (18, Asian American/Chinese) described how difficult it was
to be in China with limited Internet access when dealing with the
death of her grandmother:

[In China], I had no Internet connection at all. I wasn't able to go
on my laptop. My phone wasn't working there, so for that time, I
couldn't actually [post anything to social media]. It was annoy-
ing not being able to go off on the Internet to get away from everything else that was happening but I couldn't do anything about
it. [During my breakup in the US, I had access to social media]; I
would go on Instagram or go on Twitter or text with my friends
or watch TV or any of that to not think too much, to not let my
thoughts eat me alive.

Nancy's description of her use of social and mobile media as a
means of escape from stressful situations was common among the

participants in the US study. How people behave on social media and via their mobile device may not always be indicative of how they are feeling. People can appear as though they are "back to normal," or that they have "gotten over" their losses, but deep emotional trauma may still need to be dealt with, despite outward appearances and social media performances to the contrary.

The intimate publics of mobile media connect older practices of co-presence with newer mobile-emotive forms. Indeed, the space of posthumous performativity is only just being explored for all its complex affect (Stanyek and Piekut 2010). The various emotional textures of mobile media engagement, embodiment, and distancing involved in and around the emotional force of grief is another of the key concepts of mobile-emotive practices in this context (Rosaldo 1989). Mobile-emotive co-presence underscores our ability to understand grief as culturally, linguistically, and socially contextualized. Or as Corless et al. put it:

Grief is a response to loss or anticipated loss. Although universal, its oral and nonverbal expression varies across cultures and individuals. Loss is produced by an event perceived to be negative to varying degrees by the individuals involved and has the potential to trigger long-term changes in a person's cognitions and relationships. (2014, 132)

The goal of this book is to illustrate the ways in which mobile media now companion the bereaved in their loss. While social and mobile media allow mourners the ability to transgress their geographic or temporal contexts, the continuation of bonds places death much more into the realm of the everyday (Graham et al. 2013). This kind of active participation is often in tension with more traditional and residual norms around grief as something "private" and steeped in tradition and ritual. The generation of mobile-emotive contexts adds another dimension to the effects of online disinhibition in that users can carry these user-created imaginative, challenging, and liminal spaces *into* their everyday lives. For the active smartphone user, there is no longer a clear distinction between being online and offline. The boundaries have become quite porous and confusing, and determining what is public and what is private—what we should broadcast to others and what we should keep to ourselves—is tricky. The characterization of mobile-emotive co-presence includes the ways in which users personalize their phones (e.g., through their "wallpapers," phone cases, ringtones, etc.), the connection that they have to the content and apps stored on their phones, and how much these devices become a part of various fields of social interaction. In the next section we discuss the ways in which mobile-emotive practices allow remediated rituals to take shape.

REMEDIATED RITUALS

Many factors shape what is determined as natural and supernatural around death. Mobile media magnify both continuities and discontinuities around cultural belief and traditions. The public funeral ceremony is almost universal, yet what follows—mourning—is something that Ariès says is "understood to mean both expressions of sympathy and the style of life that custom imposed on survivors" (Ariès 1981, 511). Mobile media can be used to conjure this imaginative connection between old and new rituals surrounding death.

Mobile media remediate the relationship between media, UCC and the quotidian. By *remediate* we are deploying Bolter and Grusin's (1999) well-worn notion that highlights the haunting of older media within new media (Manovich 2001, 2003; Zynlinka and Kember 2012). This tension between old, packaged media and participatory social media in representing and disseminating information about, and emotional reaction to, significant life events will be examined in the context of the management of mobile-emotive co-presence. In many global news images, mobile media dominates both the capturing and disseminating of significant events as they unfold. We argue that while social media provides new channels for affective cultures in the form of mobile-emotive practices, it also extends to earlier media uses and rituals such as the postcard, photo album, or printed obituary.

In this book, we explore the mobile phone as part of broader remediated rituals around grief and loss. The spreadability of mobile media works to manipulate reality. While one may argue that the sharing of user-generated, emotionally charged digital content may at times be useful in raising public awareness around significant events, it often short-circuits and circumvents the real emotional needs of those who have suffered a traumatic loss. Through case studies, we will demonstrate how people now use social media to share experiences during traumatic events in ways similar to those of previous eras.

We will also see that digital data allow life and afterlife to be extended and elaborated upon in ways unimaginable in pre-online periods (Graham et al. 2013). The rise of spiritualism in the nineteenth and twentieth century will be used to set the stage for how people integrate the use of media into processing deeply emotional experiences (Schor 1994; Edmonds and Dexter 1853). The desire to continue to communicate with loved ones beyond physical death has evolved with the engagement of new media and the cultivation of a "haunted culture," which will be discussed further later in the book (Sconce 2000; Butler 2007; Partridge 2013).

Although mobile phones are promoted as devices aimed at communication and connection with others, no one can deny the isolating and intimate aspects of these devices. As constant companions, mobile devices can become our *sole* (and most desired) companions. In the context of communication in crisis, after-death communication and the continuation of bonds, companionship often rests between the individual and his or her device. Vincent points to the closeness of this relationship:

> We interact with a mobile phone in a way that we do not with other computational devices—we fondle it, we clutch it in times of crisis ready to turn to it and dial for help or solace, and we know that our loved ones are doing the same, probably at the same time. As living and ever changing sentient beings our lives are thus constantly affected by our own and others' mobile phones. (2006, 42)

The illusive feeling of connectedness fostered by frequent and, at times, superficial interaction via social and mobile media could be experienced like a haunting, a sense of presence that never truly materializes—the definition of co-presence. Creating and maintaining a virtual presence as something that transcends physical reality can help to ensure an escape from the limitations of our physical bodies, as well as a means through which we can guarantee we will never be forgotten. Having our digital content go viral can be a means of self-veneration.

The mobile-emotive conjuring of the deceased haunts us, and at times it does not feel real or appropriate. The dead may feel familiar to us but at the same time disturbing—what Freud (1917) called *unheimlich* (the uncanny). The deceased reappearing randomly via mobile media posts or through content stored on one's phone can be discomforting. Such events may not be useful to those left behind, even though we may feel somewhat drawn to such encounters (Gibson 2014). What is so intriguing about the possibility of resurrecting a digital sense of the deceased is that it is something that most people have never experienced before—and that there is strange comfort in the possibility. New experiences and new inventions breathe new life into co-occurring belief systems. The rise of spiritualism in the nineteenth and twentieth centuries coincided with the invention of electricity (Gutierrez 2003). New technology carries with it new myths and new magic. It is not by accident that James Katz (2006) dubbed the mobile phone "magic in the air."

As Stanyek and Piekut (2010) note in the case of the recorded performances of dead musicians, the digital creates a particular relationship to liveness, haunting, and co-presence. While the haunting by a musician has a genealogy in the history of recording, the digital creates a new layer of complexity in terms of the potentiality of co-present haunting. New technologies are rife with the potential to conjure imaginative ways of engaging the old with the new, the "once was" with the possibility of "what could be." Not unlike how fascination with the "magic" of electricity could allow for people to imagine an invisible realm from which illumination was possible, so too does mobile media fascinate and mesmerize us. Mobile media allow for the possibility to connect us with the illusive power of immortality and the extension of consciousness beyond our biological limitations.

CONCLUSION: DEATH'S EMOTIONAL IMPACT ON MOBILE MEDIA USE

The ways in which mobile devices become associated with loss can assist people in coming to terms with their loss, but it also has the potential to cause people to use their devices in ways that they never imagined. The ubiquitous nature of the mobile phone allows for it to be present in all moments and experiences. There are no limits to the ways in which mobile media can be integrated into our lives. The mobile-emotive experience of being "always on" (Baron 2010) is distinct from historical connections via computers. As Suler (2004) found, through computer-mediated communication—in the early days of the Internet (1990s–2000s), where being online was distinct and concrete—people in the United States were more likely to disclose personal information and act in ways that might be counter to the ways in which they would act in person. At that time, the creation of online environments allowed for many Internet users to enter these environments under a cloak of quasi-anonymity in a social domain that was experienced as devoid of outright authority or immediate social sanction. Through the use of what Suler (2004) calls "dissociative imagination" users were able to create a space that could be absent of the demands and responsibilities of everyday life. This liminal space would then serve as a form of retreat and a place where self-exploration thrived. Connecting to these online "spaces" occurred, mostly, in the comfort and privacy of one's home. And yet, the rise of the online has an uneven history globally. For example, in Japan, people leapfrogged to the mobile Internet without having a history of experiencing the online through the computer domestication phase (Ito et al. 2005; Hjorth and Arnold 2013).

Western conceptualization of the online expands upon the work of domestication approaches pioneered by Roger Silverstone (Silverstone and Haddon 1996) and then extended to computers in the work of Elaine Lally (2002). The movement of the online context from a predominantly immobile to a mobile device now further complicates the relationship between public and private, between the mutually shared and the hyperpersonal. Through the use of the mobile, as demonstrated by the US examples presented in this chapter, people can easily be led to broadcast, via social media and other online apps, intimate moments of grief and loss in seemingly quasi-private spaces. The threat of the leakage of personal information via social media and other online apps was of particular concern to the US participants. In the United States, the coveting of the privacy of one's mobile device extends to the coveting of the private nature of the content stored on one's phone. It is important to emphasize here that, despite the intention and ability built into its design to share content many American users choose not to share digital artifacts stored on their mobile devices with others. Not readily sharing important pictures of a lost loved one, in this context, indicates the ways in which using one's device as part of mourning may not necessarily mean that it is a shared experience. US participant Bianca (19, Spanish/Hispanic) reported that she did not in fact post any pictures of her grandmother to Instagram after she passed away:

> I didn't put pictures up. I think I commented on one of them, and I was tagged in a lot [of other people's pictures]. But I wasn't tagged in [any] picture of her. I was tagged in a picture of her grave, so when everyone [of my friends on social media] was like, "What is that?," I said, "Oh that's where my grandmother is buried!" But besides that, I don't like posting pictures that I am sentimental of, so mainly I just posted a picture of my mom, my younger sister, me—and not of my grandmother, even though my cousins did.

In this instance, Bianca narrated her preference for the private space generated between herself and her device. In fact, she had many pictures stored on her phone that related to her grandmother and her extended family, which she meticulously curated and put into albums. She had a preference for sharing photos via flash drives, as well as just showing people photos on her phone. She acknowledged that, for her, the public nature of social media made the sharing of sentiment appear insincere.

Mobile media's role in or association with loss can stigmatize certain devices. In a way, the technology could become contaminated by the loss and, just as with a decomposing corpse, those left behind may want to distance themselves from the offending object. Prior to her mother's death, Laila recalled looking up her mother's diagnosis on the Internet, and what she found was so traumatic that she refused to use that laptop anymore:

> I remember I Googled it. And I should have never done that because when I Googled it, I saw the worst things that I could ever see—that it was incurable and people die. And I was like "What?!" And then I remember I was on the laptop, and I think that is another reason why I don't use [the laptop] anymore, I didn't want to touch it after that, I shut it and threw it to the side and didn't want to touch it.

Laila's rejection of her device was reflective of the association she made between it and her mother's painful prognosis. Thus, associating one's mobile device with the tragic circumstances of a loss may make it difficult to use that device again. US participant Chantal (19, Jamaican) explained that her last communication with her boyfriend before he was murdered was on her cell phone. She fell asleep as she waited for him to call her back to tell her that he had arrived home safely. That call never came. Instead, she was woken by instant messages coming to her phone asking her if she was OK. She chose to ignore those messages in an attempt to deny that anything was wrong. Soon after, she completely disconnected from using mobile technology for a whole year:

> Well the phone I had when I was with him, that phone stopped working, and the charger broke and I didn't feel like I needed a phone anymore after a while, so I went without a phone for a year. I got another phone my senior year. My whole junior year

I didn't have a phone, and I really didn't want everyone, even though I did appreciate texts, I didn't want everyone to contact me that much so I just ignored my phone. And then when I tried to charge it, it wouldn't work anymore. I really didn't want to always talk about it to everyone all the time, so I kind of would ignore my phone, and my charger didn't work, so I would leave it there for over a year untouched.

It seemed that prior to her boyfriend's death, Chantal was an avid user of technology and that her active engagement with it included her connection to her boyfriend and her friends. Why else would they be reaching out to her through instant messages to her phone if they did not think that she would answer? She was on the phone with her boyfriend just prior to his murder. She offered to stay on the phone with him until he found his friend for a ride home, but he reassured her that it would be better if he could pay more attention to what was going on around him and that he would call her later. It appeared that after her boyfriend's death, she interpreted anyone else's contact with her to be intrusive and overbearing. Could it be that it was too hard for her to not receive the text messaging or the call that she most desired—the one from her boyfriend—and that all other contact was a cruel reminder of the loss?

Farah's (21, Arab/Orthodox Christian, US) best friend died while driving and attempting to read a text messaging that Farah had sent her. Farah then ceased text messaging anyone (other than the deceased— more about this later in the book). Her use of her phone shifted dramatically to only focus on her attempts at communicating with her friend via text from beyond the grave. For Hassan (18, White Muslim, US), when the older brother of his close friend died, his friend stopped using his phone. This change in his friend's mobile phone behavior

troubled Hassan and made it difficult for him to offer his friend support in his time of need. Hassan explained:

> I called him, I texted him. I am trying to connect to him through
> his cousin now— which is working better—because he is always
> with him. He is not picking up for me. Everybody else besides
> him I connect normally to, it's just him. He isolated himself
> after [his brother's death]. I just want to help him out, but he
> just isolates himself from me, and my friend was like, "just let
> him be," "let him cool down," "let him figure himself out"—but
> you just want to be there for the kid because you've known him
> for a while. I text him, I call him—I think he just left his phone
> at home. He doesn't touch it. I don't think he has it with him.
> Usually he answers text[s], and usually he texts me first.

Hassan was distressed about the way in which his friend's use of his
mobile device changed after the loss of his brother. His expressed
concern was motivated by his desire to offer support and to companion his friend through his grief. But the change was also distressing because it made it obvious that something had happened to his
friend, that his friend was changed by the loss in some way, and this
interrupted or suspended his connection to Hassan. Hassan then
fluctuated between wanting to respect this distance and the privacy
of his friend on the one hand, and his desire to be a part of the rituals
to honor his friend's brother and to show respect to his family on the
other.

The evidence from the US interviews provided in this chapter
contextualizes and elucidates the mobile-emotive. Throughout this
book we will use this term to represent the mobile as a vehicle through
which deeply affective experiences are represented and made "real."
Having outlined the context for this book and the specific issues

CO-PRESENT RECONSTRUCTIONS OF DEATH, LOSS, AND MOURNING

relating to studying mobile media and grief as a dynamic, culturally specific process, we now move on to the book's Section I, "Mobile-Emotive Rituals." In this section of the book we have three chapters that explore mobile-emotive rituals specific to grief and mourning. Through intimate stories of grief in and through mobile media practices, we make sense of how this media is entangling our rituals in ways that are both part of a continuum and also a disruption of it.

SECTION I

MOBILE-EMOTIVE RITUALS

Companionship

During the actual floods [in Victoria, Australia, 2011], my mobile did not leave my side, but it was more for documentation purposes (we had no coverage). I was documenting for insurance purposes (little did I know), but also I think that my personal history with the mobile phone plays a role here, too. These types of events involve a huge loss of voice and control. I think the methodical use of my camera phone gave me a sense of control, and gradually replaced the anger I felt alongside the psychological loss. I created my own organic transitions here; it was very empowering to generate both personal and community-driven memorials for these kinds of experiences/events. As I am a poet and artist, this was a natural direction for me to take with my own recovery journey. (Performance artist and poet Klare Lanson, interviewed in 2015)

When the Australian performance artist and poet Klare Lanson lost her house in regional Victoria to the devastating floods of 2011, she was overcome with fear and grief. As the floodwater subsided, it was in the trauma of the aftermath that Klare attempted to rebuild her life. The feeling of loss and voicelessness through the experience of the disaster saw the mobile phone play a key role in her sense of resilience. Despite the phone *literally* not working, it played a role *symbolically* to give her a sense of voice through the visualization tool of the camera phone. Throughout the whole process, the phone rarely left her hand.

Rather than being overwhelmed by grief, Lanson decided to redeploy and channel the trauma and loss of the event into a community-building exercise that intertwined the online with the offline. Playing with the idea of the cloud as a digital metaphor that also has offline and physical dimensions, she interviewed affected community members about their experiences and processes of recovery. This project became *#wanderingcloud*. Figure 3.1 depicts the *#wanderingcloud* website. Through the use of mobile media and its growing relationship to cloud computing, *#wanderingcloud* explored the entangling of the online and offline in the grieving process. Here Lanson used the metaphor of cloud computing to explore the grief left by weather clouds. By collaging and montaging moments and gestures in and around the trauma of the floods, *#wanderingcloud* provided a poetic

Figure 3.1 *#wanderingcloud* website.

way in which to consider how the entanglement between the online and offline is changing how we understand memorialization.

In this chapter, we investigate the shifting role of memorialization through case studies of individual usage of mobile and social media to harness and bring together family and friends channeling positive ways for perpetual co-present memorialization. The mobile phone is an active part of everyday life for many, and as such it provides a pivotal role in the construction and maintenance of memorialization. This chapter will explore how the sense of co-presence generated through use of mobile-emotive rituals and practices can be experienced as a form of companionship and continuing bond. As we see from Lanson's traumatic experience during the 2011 floods, mobile media can function within various literal and symbolic dimensions. Drawing on fieldwork predominantly undertaken in Australia, this chapter considers how the mobile phone can facilitate a kind of constant companionship that can be a lifesaver in times of extreme emotional suffering, and can assist users in practical as well as affective/effective aspects of the grieving process.

This chapter will also focus on the role that ritual plays in the cultivation and maintenance of mobile-emotive companionship during periods of emotional distress. We show that mobile media has the capacity to continue bonds and emotional attachments both literally (as a communication device) and symbolically. The symbolic dimension is seen in the opening vignette, in which the typical function of Lanson's phone becomes dysfunctional, but its power as both witness and companion of trauma still lies within the device itself (Marwick and Ellison 2012).

Examples from our fieldwork in this and the following chapters will explore how the use of mobile devices in the context of mobile-emotive companionship can ease the process of planning, preparing, and participating in ritual, as well as the ways in which it can complicate and undermine the intention of such rituals. Whether it is through receiving condolence messages or revisiting shared memories through photos and other forms of digital memorials, mobile-emotive mourning rituals and their ability to provide a sense of companionship can be comforting at times. For Scott H. Church, digital memorials can help us to understand "the ways in which the digital sphere has disrupted or altered material and aesthetic displays of death and the associated genre of discourses surrounding death" (2013, 184). As Church notes,

> [The] new phenomenon of digital memorializing displays a curious interplay between the discourses of material (permanent) death displays and the ephemeral memorializing (pseudo-permanence) of Internet culture. Facebook, MySpace, Virtual Eternity, and MyDeathSpace are a few examples of websites that enable continued "dialogue" between the mortal and post-mortal by allowing "interaction" with the deceased . . . In the digital culture of remembrance, then, these social network sites function as spaces of remembrance, efficient vehicles to distribute messages to a mass audience, and loci for the mediated construction of affiliation in a community of bereavement. (184)

Yet, the management of one's perpetual, ever-present, mobile-emotive connections at such a sad time can also feel burdensome and "unnatural." As mentioned in the previous chapter, users may experience a desire to "pull the plug" on their devices when the reality of loss disrupts how they typically utilize mobile media.

To explore the role of ritual around grief through mobile media, this chapter firstly discusses the history of rituals around death and loss, especially from anthropology. Here ritual can be understood as a situated cultural practice. After outlining the history of definitions of ritual, the chapter explores some examples of ritual in and around mobile media memorialization. Here we embed theories of ritual within the empirical experiences of contemporary life to think about its continuities and discontinuities. We finish with a further discussion of the #wanderingcloud project, assessing how this collaborative art project explored mobile media and loss in a variety of ways.

A SHORT HISTORY OF RITUAL

There have been attempts to compartmentalize death and remembering into discrete memorial online sites, but this has, for the most part, failed, since it is within the messy place of the social (whether social media or not) that grief is played out, performed, and experienced. Early studies into social media (online) memorials revealed struggles against social norms that have haunted users (Marwick and Ellison 2012; Brubaker and Hayes 2011; Brubaker et al. 2012). In "The Digital Remains," Jessa Lingel uses Facebook's policies to provide a "springboard for reflecting on the online grief as a social phenomenon." She argues:

> The sophisticated tools and applications developed by social network sites (SNS) have enabled users to interact in more varied and more efficient ways, but the development of technical and cultural protocols for handling the virtual identities of recently deceased users has lagged, raising culturally complex questions of what should happen to individuals' online identities after death. These tensions become legible in Facebook's evolving policies for digital remains of deceased members and the reactions of the user community. (2013, 190)

As Lingel observes, these tensions are part of broader offline issues around the movement of death and grief into the mundane and everyday. For Lingel, the movement into social media DIY mourning represents both a "technological practice and a social one," highlighting the need to shift policies in and around understanding digital remains. Understanding the online as a continuation of the offline is important in this shift. As Klassens, Groote, and Vanclay (2013) note, the often "private" place of mourning can be recontextualized and transformed through public space practices. In their study, they focus upon permanent roadside memorials in which mourners transform the death site into a "place of care." They make this observation:

> Establishing private memorials in public spaces brings death into the public sphere. This process runs counter to the trend in Western societies of being death-denying, where the public expression of grief is essentially taboo, and death sequestered, which is removed from the public sphere into the individual's private world. . . . Boundaries between the public and private sphere have changed and the emotional repressiveness of many Western societies has gradually given way to greater expressiveness in public mourning, as is evident in response to the passing of famous people, disasters, and roadside tributes (2013, 146).

The rendering public of what once was deemed intimate is a process embedded in mobile media practices. By traversing the online with the offline, the intimate with the public, mobile media partake in more broadly changing rituals around memorialization as they create reflections and interventions on these practices. Mobile media practices allow both informal and official memorialization processes to occur, and to move in and out of the mundanities of everyday life. Mobile media remediate older media practices and material cultures by application to mourning rituals, while also demonstrating emergent forms of visuality and mobile-emotive co-presence. While mobile devices allow for access to social media sites, the devices themselves become the sites of interaction with the digital content they store.

On the one hand, mobile media can be understood as part of broader media contexts of being "online" in the experience of ritual, specifically the rituals surrounding grief and mourning. On the other hand, mobile media have specific affordances that shape the content in ways that are as intimate and personal as they are public. As Brubaker, Hayes, and Dourish note, social media "enable expansion—temporally, spatially, and socially—of public mourning. Rather than looking at online practices as disruptions of traditional practices of grief and memorialization . . . [they] are new sites in which public mourning takes place" (2013, 152). Mobile phone use is highly ritualized, personalized, and customized. It is then the personal nature of the devices and the rendering of the content stored on the mobile device as extensions of the users' emotional worlds that then allows for these devices to be used to generate mobile-emotive practices and rituals. This reality of everyday mobile phone use facilitates its integration into other kinds of ritualized behaviors. Rituals are a part of the grieving process. We use the definition of ritual in the context of grief in similar ways to the work of Kenneth J. Doka. As such, ritual "is defined as highly symbolic acts that confer transcendental significance and meaning on certain life events or experiences" (Doka 2002, 135). This definition allows for acts that may be shared with others, as well as those that are performed by individuals alone.

Rituals become the vehicle through which people can contain as well as express emotion. The devices become companions in ritual and help to foster a *liminal* space through which a sense of mobile-emotive co-presence can be rendered as part of grieving a loss. Beyond the importance of death rituals in promoting resilience and restoring social order, rituals serve a psychological purpose as well. Rituals often provide a space, both physical and psychological, where transitions can take place. Van Gennep (2013) described this as a *liminal* space, in that people encounter rituals at the threshold of consciousness, whereby participation may not be fully comprehended, yet still deeply felt (Doka, 2002).

Rituals are sites of imagination for those engaged in their construction and performance. As such, rituals can be used to promote meaning-making related to loss (Hall 2001). They legitimize emotional expression related to grief and loss and allow for a sense of doing or acting upon the grief so as to produce an emotionally cathartic effect. Doka (2002, 143) described rituals as providing "a structure for events fraught with ambivalence (e.g., anniversaries), allowing individuals to reframe events or experiences, and offering support and symbolic mastery. Rituals also transcend time. They can mark distinct points in the grieving process, allowing grieving people to meet their different needs."

Ritual has a long, complicated history in both anthropology and sociology. In particular, the field of the anthropology of death has conducted much of the research into rituals and grief. For key ritual scholar Catherine Bell (1992, 19), ritual is seen as a performance of conceptual orientations. In her seminal work, *Ritual Theory, Ritual Practice*, Bell argues that ritual is used in a community to create a collective set of beliefs or ideals. For Bell, within the dynamism of culture and societal change, ritual provides a bridge between tradition and constant social change (20). Bell's model of ritual has three elements: ritual as an activity, ritual as dynamism between thought and activity, and the dichotomy between actor and thinker (31).

For Bell, ritual performs and enacts a system of symbols by integrating the conceptual and dispositional. As such, ritual is viewed as a "cultural performance" (1992, 37) that is "dramatized" (38). Bell's theorization around a practiced notion of ritual is important in our study, which seeks to explore rituals in and around mobile media and loss. Here the mobile phone can help to create a bridge between tradition and social change. It can be part of ritual as an activity, it can be present between thought and activity, and it can mediate between the feelings and the acting (and enacting) of the cultural performance.

Informing Bell's notions of ritual is undoubtedly the work of Robert Hertz. Hertz, as mentioned previously, is viewed as one of the key anthropologists of death. Like his teacher Émile Durkheim, Hertz focused upon the *social aspects* of death rather than its biological or psychological aspects. It is important to note that Durkheim's book *Suicide* (1951) radically transformed how death and sociological research were conceptualized, and that this unquestionably had an impact upon Hertz. According to Hertz, human death thoughts and rituals are primarily social products whereby the deceased enters the imagined world "which each society constructs in its own image" (Hertz 1960, 79). For Hertz, the most important function of death rituals is to promote the reorganization of the social order and the restoration of faith, which have been challenged by the bereavement process and by the loss itself.

Hertz's work on death is important in understanding that grief is something informed by cultural context, and that it is an ongoing process—as opposed to the limited Western definitions of grief that have viewed it as something to get over (Rosenblatt 1996). Hertz's work on death draws from his fieldwork in Indonesia, where he noted that death was not an event but a process. Hertz's work emphasized death as part of transition in the process of life. As he noted in the context of the Olo Ngaju, "death . . . is . . . not a singular event occurring only once in the history of the individual, it is an episode that repeats itself endlessly and that merely marks the passage from one form of existence to another" (Hertz 1960, 61). Death not only involves the physical body, but also the blotting of a social identity. "When a person dies, the society loses in him much more than a unit; it is stricken in the very principle of its life, in the faith it has in itself" (71). Ritual is a collective response to this attack. For Arnold van Gennep (2013), rituals performed at death parallel other rituals in critical periods in the life of the individual, such as birth, social puberty, or marriage. He calls these "rites of passage" in which social order is reconfirmed.

For Bronislaw Malinowski, ritual and religion sought to make sense of the anxiety and irrationality caused "by the real tragedies of human life, out of the conflict between human plans and realities" (2005, 71). "The existence of strong personal attachments and the fact of death, which of all human events is the most upsetting and disorganizing to man's calculations, are perhaps the main sources of religious belief" (71). Johannes Fabian ([1973] 2004) took a reflexive look at the anthropological study of death in his essay "How Others Die: Reflections on the Anthropology of Death." He argued that earlier discussions of death within anthropology tended towards parochialization, folklorization, and exoticization. Fabian wanted anthropology to focus upon the social construction of death to suggest three possible directions: a processual, practice-orientated view of cultural conceptions of death; a dialectical model of the sociocultural reality of death, paying equal attention to the individual and social realities; and a communicative, language-centered approach to death and dying.

More recently the field of the anthropology of death has seen publications such as Peter Metcalf and Richard Huntington's *Celebrations of Death: The Anthropology of Mortuary* (1991), which draws on fieldwork to address key questions about death culture research (emotional reaction to death; symbolic associations of death, etc.). In Milton Cohen's *Death Ritual: Anthropological Perspectives*, Cohen argues that "ritual is behavior"—it is "religion in action". He goes on to note that rituals are "personal and private behavior, as it is social (as cited in Wallace 1966, 102)." During the Victorian era, in the West, mourning became more social and almost trendy, with various types of clothing and accessories that were expected to be worn by the bereaved (especially by those of the upper classes). Beyond the funeral, the cemetery, and other rituals and rites, the process of mourning became public.

Traditions surrounding public mourning continue, as many cultures throughout the world observe mourning as a social event. It is rare that grief rituals involve mourning by one's self. A death marks a distinction between the living and the dead. Grief thrusts the living into an almost in-between state. Tangible representations of this marked transition and change in one's life and communal structure are steeped in tradition. How people use their mobile devices during this time is also reflective of this transitional space between the living, the dead, and the bereaved. Much of the important past work on the anthropology of death didn't need to negotiate the role of the online, and especially mobile media, in interweaving social practices. When thinking about contemporary practice, it becomes apparent that a functionalist approach, as in Erving Goffman's interactional ritual, which focuses on Western notions of face symbolism, neglects to understand some of the more complex social processes at play, as suggested in the work of Hertz and Bell.

In the transition of anthropological studies into online memorialization and death, there has been a focus on online-specific concepts—such as "thanatechnology"—to link contemporary practices with earlier ones (Kalan 2015). Much of this work focuses on Facebook as a problematic signifier for global social media, cancelling out the different affordances of how Facebook operates across mobile and nonmobile media, as well as countries that do not use Facebook, such as China, where Weibo and WeChat dominate, or Japan, where LINE dominates. As Molly Kalan (2015) argues in her thanatechnology study of online memorialization and Facebook, when someone dies we differentiate between the biological death and the social lives of the material objects associated with that person to partake in the memory process. According to Kalan,

> We give ourselves the task of maintaining the social identity of the deceased and postponing social death as long as possible. Contributing to the memorialized Facebook page is a key part of keeping social identity alive, but it ultimately allows and perhaps invites us to ignore the reality of biological death and oblivion. (2015, n.p.)

Kalan's morality fable juxtaposes the maintaining of living memories online with the denial of biological death. However, this simplifies the process and ritual of remembering and memorialization to something lesser than the actual "life" of the deceased. Instead, in this book we seek to explore how rituals around memorialization operate in a Hertzian sense to construct society "in its own image" (Hertz 1960, 79). Through these death rituals, social order and faith is revisited. In the next section, we explore fieldwork conducted in Melbourne, Australia, with participants who had experienced losing a loved one in the past five years. We explore some of the contradictions at play whereby mobile media can partly amplify the importance of the memorialization process while also creating a sense of distance and multiplicity between the bereaved as a collective group. Often these two conflicting experiences can operate in unison and are not easily reconciled.

CONSTANTLY ON HAND: MOBILE MEDIA AS THE WIRELESS LEASH

Michael Arnold (2004), in his early work on phenomenological readings of the mobile phone, described it as "Janus-faced." Deploying the Greek myth to describe mobile media's multiple paradoxes, he noted that mobile media was a wireless leash that both set us free (to move) and created new accountabilities and expectations. The mobile phone traverses both personal and public, work and leisure, in new ways. Jack Qiu (2009) later defined these mobile media paradoxes in terms of being a wireless leash. Melissa Gregg (2011) characterized this pushing and pulling in terms of work/life "bleeding," where mobile media constantly bleed contexts, modes of presence, and media.

The paradoxical pushing and pulling, blurring and bleeding, are magnified in the case of dealing with mobile-emotive grief, companionship, and remembering. The online amplifies offline feelings, emotions, gestures, and sentiment. It can also, by traversing different spatialities and temporalities, virtually bring together people who are geographically separated, while at the same time create psychological distance between those who are in close physical proximity. In this section, we explore the different ways in which the pros and cons of online and mobile media can play out in terms of mobile-emotive companionship and the ensuing rituals surrounding loss.

Our first case study is with Jeremy, who lost his lifelong best friend, Tim, two years ago. Both Jeremy and Tim are part of "Generation Y," a generation often referred to as "Millennials," and also often defined as "digital natives." They are well versed in mobile and social media. So when Jeremy lost Tim to suicide in 2013, family and friends used mobile and social media to keep in constant contact, and to provide a space in which Tim could be present through memories and memorialization processes. As noted in Chapter 2, much of the research into online memorialization has concentrated upon the positive impact of the online context to overcome temporal and spatial boundaries (Brubaker, Hayes, and Dourish 2013; Graham et al. 2015). However, the displacement of boundaries posed by the online can also create problems. For Jeremy (32, Jewish-Australian), the role of online media in the memorialization processes was not only ambiguous but also possibly negative. Jeremy stated,

> Facebook is the main offender; it changes everything, it is different than nondigital, it's both good and bad. It helped me in the short term, but as time wears on it is less useful, even possibly detrimental, for me anyway.

When asked for further elaboration, Jeremy noted,

> Facebook was the big one for us (a whole lot of us who were writing eulogies actually started a private group so we could share notes, and the eulogies are still on there) and on Tim's birthday and the anniversary of his death people post from and post to his still-active account. Both of those dates are coming up in the next few months, so more will appear there shortly. . . . I think online/mobile media does change the grieving and memorialization processes. For me, because I live so far away from the group, it was really helpful in terms of the time between death and funeral, and also for a time after I got back from NSW. When no one here really understood what I was feeling (or at least, not about Tim directly), I could jump onto FB [Facebook] or call/text a friend and we'd just go for it, tell funny stories and cry or whatever.

As Jeremy spoke about the role of mobile-emotive companionship to help overcome distance, especially when his family and friends were in another Australian state, he also noted that the online could exasperate the distance and loneliness:

> Again, because I'm far away from the group, I get a call on anniversaries, and I participate in the parties on the phone. I was sent

one of Tim's shot-glasses in the mail, so for his birthday I call the crew, and we all have a drink together, then over the next day or two people send me photos of the party and I get a bit of a kick out of it. But at the same time, I also feel really distant, and sometimes the sharing actually makes me feel a bit isolated, less a part than apart. It reminds me that I'm not there to help out, or whatever, and I end up feeling pretty rubbish for a few days. I don't want to call or FB message anyone because that's where the problem comes from, but I also really want to get in touch because they're the people that get it.

For Jeremy, online social media as mobile-emotive companionship meant there was never closure:

It's a lot like a messy breakup, where your partner hasn't collected all their stuff, so you keep finding things that remind you of them and it makes the whole thing harder to move past. Sort of, because sometimes it's the opposite, and when you're feeling really alone finding that old love letter or hair-tie or whatever reminds you that you were in love at one point, and that makes you feel good, too. It's a lot of back and forth.

As Jeremy noted, the type of death is important in the grieving and memorialization processes. Suicide leaves a different type of grief for the deceased's loved ones, including a terrible sense of guilt. When it is remembered online, the focus upon suicide and the negative press it attracts can take the focus. Jeremy put it this way:

Tim's death (from suicide) has been really different from the rest because it's so dense in terms of social media, whereas the others I've dealt with have been pretty low on that agenda. We do funerals, do wakes, and it's gone, but this one isn't like that at all. The extra, or ongoing connection is a bit of a double-edged sword. I guess generally I prefer just getting everything out of my system so I can move on, but I'm really aware that other people aren't like that, so sometimes I'm almost forced to relive things or contribute so that I either don't appear callous or because other people want me to, maybe even need me to add something.

Through the simultaneous use of mobile media like text messaging, IM, and MMS, along with Facebook, Jeremy and his friends and family were able to sustain constant contact in the days following Tim's death. Mobile and online media were used to share thoughts about what the eulogy should say as well as providing support to one another. They shared photos of their deceased friend on Facebook and discussed the upcoming wake. For friends who couldn't attend the wake or be physically there for the family, social media provided ways they could record their thoughts and wishes (as depicted in Figure 3.2).

At times like birthdays, Facebook would become a place to share the ongoing memories. When the deceased is a young person, events are used to reflect upon the sadness of life, with its often unfair situations. Through the regret and loss, shared messages of love can help not only keep the continuing bonds going but also allow for the understanding of grief as never-ending within intimate public settings. People can revisit, reflect, and choose their own time to respond.

The online comments on Tim's Facebook feed were often filled with sadness and loss, as well as people trying to remember the positive things to preserve his memory, as depicted in Figure 3.3. Sometimes, posts included photos from visiting the grave. Tim's Facebook account continued, recording and sharing messages between friends and family. Facebook operated like a memorial specter whereby the pages are haunted by multiple forms of mobile-emotive companionship, co-presence, and absence.

Kat⬛⬛⬛⬛⬛.   8/29, 10:36pm

Hi guys, Please excuse this MSG being via Facey, but I just
wanted to send you all a hug (virtually) and this was the
best way I could think of since I am away and can't be there
tomorrow. I know how close you all were with Tim, at
various points and degrees throughout school and after.
Losing someone is never easy ~ situations like this are
even harder. It feels almost surreal. He was such a great
guy and I don't think I'll ever forget that big grin he always
had ~ so many great memories from school and after.
Sending you all love, light and strength for tomorrow ~
hopefully see you all soon xo much love Katie xo

——————————— September 1, 2013 ———————————

Jon⬛⬛⬛⬛⬛   9/1, 12:18am

Cheers babe. You missed a pretty awesome day (all things
considered).

Figure 3.2 Ghosting presence: Facebook as intimate co-presence.

9 friends **posted** on Timothy's timeline for his birthday.

Tim⬛⬛⬛⬛⬛
Birthday: July 17

Write a birthday wish on his Timeline...

Jame⬛⬛⬛⬛ ▸ Tim⬛⬛⬛⬛
July 19, 2014 · 👥

Miss you buddy

Like · Comment

Write a comment...

M⬛⬛⬛⬛ ▸ Timo⬛⬛⬛⬛
July 18, 2014 · 👥

Happy birthday Timbo...I'm having an Irish beer for you! Xoxo miss you.

Figure 3.3 Happy Birthday wishes to Tim on Facebook.

The sharing of pictures from the physical gravesite, as depicted in Figure 3.4, also allowed loved ones to be present in multiple forms of memorialization. A visit by a friend and then a shared posting can be used to rekindle and share the pain and the loss. Through the multiple channels offered by Facebook, IM, text messaging, and MMS, grieving loved ones were able to construct multiple intimate publics in which to share their ongoing grief. However, for Jeremy these multiple intimate publics often meant that grief bled across these sites and interrupted him throughout the day. Constantly being online and mobile also means that we are open to other people's grieving processes at all

Figure 3.4 A shared picture of fresh flowers at Tim's grave.

times. Unlike the "closure" of funerals or wakes, in which open grieving is expected to be contained and then limited to or attached to specific places, social and mobile media keep those spaces and places "open" across different subjectivities, spatialities, and temporalities. This opening effect of social media can have both positive and negative results.

In the next case study, we meet cousins Sophie (40, Anglo-Australian) and Catherine (28, Anglo-Australian) in Melbourne, Australia. When Sophie's brother John unexpectedly died of a heart attack, Catherine set up a Facebook tribute page to remember him. Titled "In Loving Memory of," Catherine, a competent Facebook user, posted tributes on John's Facebook page. Sophie held John's phone constantly, as if he were still alive in there. Looking at the text messaging, e-mails, Facebook, and Google Maps, Sophie felt like she could recount John's last days, the places and spaces he visited both online and offline. She revisited the mobile traces constantly. At the same time, the mobile phone was used as a way to contact John's friends and work colleagues to let them know about John passing away. Text messaging was used so that the receivers could process the news in their own time. The Facebook tribute page, which linked to John's personal page, was also used to source images of John from friends and family for use at the funeral.

The generational divide in media usage was heightened when it became apparent that John's mother, heavily traumatized, was out of the media loop about events, friends, and messages. Sophie would have to print out the Facebook pages so her mother could read the text and look at the pictures. As the years wore on, John's Facebook page would go through ebbs and flows. On anniversaries, such as the day of his death or his birthday, messages would fill the page. Then silence. Then someone who didn't know John had died would find out and share their disbelief and grief. Every so often, John's ex-wife would leave inappropriate messages and John's family would try and ignore them. Here the intimacy was heightened at the same time as it flattened. Some participants would overshare their feelings, while others who assumed they were closer to the deceased would be left numb.

In the case of mourning processes, invisible symbolic actions can be left unnoticed by the ocular-centrism of social media. Uneven patterns of use, along with the array of different, often tacit, expectations and rituals, become sites for misunderstanding in times of grief. This is magnified in the case of loved ones "stewarding" deceased digital data as they witness different degrees of performativity of intimacy, which doesn't always collate with the actual closeness to the deceased (Brubaker 2016).

Like Jeremy's feelings, Sophie felt a sense of ambivalence towards the commemorative Facebook tribute page as a tool for mobile-emotive companionship. She would often visit it, much like the gravesite, and reflect. Unlike the gravesite, where she would leave flowers, on the Facebook page she would just virtually sit there. For Catherine, the mobile media traces allowed her to "feel" that John was still there. Therefore she stayed with an "old" smartphone out of fear that the text messages on her phone might be erased if she upgraded. She noted,

> I have his phone that I often look at, as if trying to find bits about his life I didn't know. It's like a mystery. I feel like if I could know everything he felt and experienced, somehow the pain would be less. I have a really old smartphone. Very few apps work on it. But I can't upgrade. Not yet. I'm worried that it will erase him and his messages. A new phone represents a type of "moving on" which I'm not ready to engage with. I don't think I'll ever be ready.

This sentimentality toward the phone has multiple dimensions. It's not just the digital traces inside. It's the materiality. And also what that materiality symbolizes in daily rituals. For Sophie, the traces of her brother on digital media like Facebook are positive because they keep him alive through memories. She noted,

> Every so often a new person wants to join his Facebook tribute page. It means I can gain a sense into a new dimension of his life, as if he were still living. Not many people post except at key dates like his birthday or the date of his death. However, I do get annoyed by one person [the ex-girlfriend] on the page that acts as if she knew my brother best. She always gets on the page and rants and raves. I want to block her, but then I realize she has pain, too. But it goes to show that those who might be most verbal and public in their demonstrations might not actually be the ones who are experiencing it the deepest.

For Sophie, the lingering of her brother through his digital traces allowed his memory to live on. Every day she "sees" her brother via Facebook or text messaging on her phone. This seeing is an important part of keeping his memory alive. When asked about backing up the "ephemeral" material of him on her phone, she said,

> I know the material on the phone is ephemeral. It can be lost easily. And yet the idea of transferring it to a computer to store all the memories of him defeats the point. It's because the mobile phone is always with me and so intimate that it's important the images and messages stay on there. It means I can always check and look at them. If they were on a computer, they wouldn't feel the same. There would be distance. It would be like they were "filed away." It would be as if I should "move on." I don't need to move on because I want his memory to live on.

In this section, we have explored some of the ways in which digital and specifically mobile media can extend the process of ritual in and around remembering loved ones who have passed away. We see how mobile media, from Facebook tribute pages to saved text messages and camera phone images, allow participants pathways to ritual and emotional ties during the undulating processes of grief and loss. In the case of Jeremy, we see that the particular performativity of social media such as Facebook distorts the levels of intimacy and amplifies the distance.

For Catherine and Sophie, mobile media is representative of continuing bonds whereby the mobile phone is much like carrying a picture or letter in the wallet. We carry it around everywhere we go and are perpetually reminded of the importance of the deceased. It grounds grief and memorialization in the everyday. In the next section, we will revisit the example of performance artist/poet Klare Lanson. Here we can think about the creative and expressive dimensions of mobile-emotive companionship in helping with processes of loss and recovery through collaboration and sharing stories.

#WANDERINGCLOUD: THE ART OF LOSS

When I think deeply about it [the trauma of the house flood] in my own psychology, I recall climbing up my back cliff in the middle of the night to escape from the fast-rising floodwaters. I had my son in one arm, my laptop over my shoulder, and I held my mobile with the other, using it as a torch. This image still resonates with me. I felt very isolated and scared, and think this is why location media also resonates with me; it overtly connects experiences, especially events where loss of some kind occurs. This has to be a good thing, and can be seen as an important role this kind of technology plays. I think the role is very different to nondigital ways of memorialization. It takes the concept of a memorial away from patriarchal modes relating to location, allowing us to "remember" within the organic framework that memory operates and constantly shifts within. (Lanson interview, 2015)

As noted in the chapter introduction, Klare Lanson made the work *#wanderingcloud* to conceptually explore her regional communities' thoughts and responses to the 2011 Victorian flood event. Consisting of three stages, *#wanderingcloud* involved researching local flood history and collecting and recording stories from the community; remixing these digital stories and related field recordings into soundscapes (sometimes using iPhone apps), which were then uploaded to the digital "cloud" (see Figure 3.5 for examples of the images uploaded to #wanderingcloud); and then inviting Brisbane-based artists Clocked Out Duo and local artists Jacques Soddell and

Figure 3.5 *#wanderingcloud* images.

Figure 3.6 *#wanderingcloud*: mobile media shots of the live performance, Castlemaine Arts Festival, 2015.

Andree Cozens to respond to these online soundscapes creatively in live performance (see Figure 3.6 for mobile media shots of the live performance). Lanson also invited other flood victims (also creative practitioners) she met during the data collection period to join the live performance events, creating yet another metaphorical 'cloud'. As she noted,

> Conceptually, the project investigates how this community data can be exchanged and presented as a "geographical" sound map

and performance work. The "traces" of connectivity that occur transform into a unique form of collective thinking, a trickle-down effect—a soundscape made up of voices, imagery, and psychological triggers (e.g., rain). This layered and often subconscious community response is a thing of beauty, and I believe vital to the health and well-being of both individual and a broader regional community.

When asked about mobile media use, Lanson observed that "the use of online and mobile media as a form of memorialization works well for me, as it's as organic and static as the processes involved with loss and grief." She continued,

> I cannot remember a period of time when I did not use my mobile as a weird form of memorialization, for both the process of my personal loss and also to drive momentum for the communities, their loss, and attaching to the project itself. It also seems strangely related to some kind of "digital proof," something for memory to latch onto in space-time, to share with others. The poetics of the "memorial" has changed, too. As we learn, we change. Memorialization should represent this and I think digital media does this successfully. After all, our memory is not static is it?

Lanson went on to note that the physical and psychological are deeply entangled. In the loss of voice encountered, Lanson found that utilizing online—and especially mobile media—helped to provide a ritualized space for conceptualizing this grief into a community process. Lanson's *#wanderingcloud* reminds us of Bell's definition of ritual as a device to create a collective set of beliefs or ideals. Ritual becomes the bridge between tradition and social change. In the case of the devastating experience of the floods for Lanson and her community, it was the mobile phone—not as a functional phone, but rather as an extension of the camera (and sound in live performance)—that served to document and also companion Lanson (and her son) through the trauma. As she noted,

> In terms of loss and grief, natural disasters are not really about the physical loss that inevitably occurs. Sure, the physical loss can be traumatic, but what's more important is the psychological; the loss of voice and not being able to personalize aspects of grief about this loss within small communities. Communities who did not have a voice during this time, and who also received minimal support from outside their physical location.

CONCLUSION: MOBILE-EMOTIVE RITUALS OF COMPANIONSHIP

In this chapter, we have explored the role of rituals in and around mobile media practices in times of loss and grief. As we have demonstrated in this chapter, these rituals can be paradoxical—linking to tradition, on the one hand, and to social change, on the other. In this paradox, mobile media operates both literally and symbolically to extend our continuing bonds. In the case of Jeremy, we saw how mobile and online media can amplify both a sense of proximity and distance via mobile-emotive companionship in times of grief. For Catherine and Sophie, mobile media allowed John's afterlife to be extended, which provided much comfort.

However, at times, vocal friends appeared more intimate with John in his afterlife than they were while he was alive. For example, the ex-girlfriend's perpetual demonstrations of knowing John on Facebook only served to highlight to Sophie how much the ex-girlfriend didn't know. It also demonstrated how the complexity of one person is mapped upon the digital through multiple and conflicting interpretations. Yet Sophie didn't feel it was right to block her, since everyone has to experience their grief differently—some more publicly than others.

In the next chapter, we continue to explore the role of mobile-emotive rituals around affirmation and intensification. Drawing on fieldwork in the United States, the chapter investigates individual rituals in and around loss and how these practices contribute to mobile media memorialization.

4

Affirmation and Intensification

Truthfully, I signed up for the study because it amazes me how the family dealt with the death through social media and I didn't. [My aunt] wasn't dead [for] an hour before they had it up on Facebook, and I was so angry because I thought it was so personal—they were tweeting and just sending pictures of her, and I was so angry by that. Because instead of being with the family, they were on social media letting everyone know how she had died and conversating [*sic*] with everyone else, and it wasn't just me [that had a problem with it], it was other family members who are not involved in [social media]. We were really turned off by it. (Nadine, 39, Black, US)

New mobile-emotive habits around grief often rub against traditional practices in unexpected ways, highlighting different, often tacit etiquette and literacies around mobile media. In line with the case studies from the previous chapter, participants in the US study did indicate that the integration of mobile and social media into the mourning process put a new kind of pressure on them to "do grief" in a more public way. Some participants were made uncomfortable, and yet they were still intrigued by these new mobile media practices. Not all participants readily embraced new forms of memorialization and ritual around death and bereavement emerging from new media. Some expressed how the new expectations around public grief via social media tended to contradict aspects of their own self-narrative. The pressure to "do grief" online was interpreted as a kind of performance that seemed to benefit others more than those directly impacted by the loss. As US participant Rangani (20, Sri Lankan, Buddhist) explained, when her friend lost her dad in Sri Lanka, the ways in which her school friends (in Sri Lanka) acknowledged the loss on their more public WhatsApp chat felt intrusive and almost rude:

> We have another group on WhatsApp with like six other girls . . . so one of those girls changed the group icon to a white flag[1] once [our friend's] dad passed away, and we knew that our friend wouldn't like that at all because — even though [the girl] did it thinking [it was] good — we were like, "Oh my god!" [and] "She is not making her feel any better at all!"—all of a sudden she just changed the icon to a white flag, making it very obvious [that a loss had occurred]. So we were waiting for two or three days to pass so we could change the icon. Because over time [our friend who lost her dad] probably goes on the phone, she is like looking at it, and it kind of reminds her [of her loss], so we wanted to [change it]. The girl [who changed the icon] was sincere but she wasn't that close, for some reason it felt like she was doing something rude! As soon as she changed the icon, we all got a notification that she changed it. One of my friends sent me a private message saying "Did you see?" Then after three days I changed the icon right away [laughs].

In Rangani's case, the pressure to share feelings and details of loss online appeared to be less about sharing genuine concern for

---

1. In Sri Lanka, when there is a funeral, mourners put out the white flag, and everything is white in the funeral. The body is dressed in white, everything is white, and everyone comes wearing white. Changing the icon to a white flag is thus a symbol of acknowledging the loss.

the bereaved and more about friends' expectations around how to respond in a WhatsApp chat when a friend's loved one dies. It was about how the bereaved must now allow space for others to be "good friends" (Facebook or otherwise) to them and to perform that "goodness" in a public way, oftentimes now on social media or group messaging. The public display aspect of offering condolences appeared to some participants as more of a spectacle, as in Rangani's story. Some participants did not like feeling at the center of this kind of attention, nor did they want to experience this grief as something that would change how people saw them or interacted with them. US participant Maureen (18, White) did not feel comforted by her ability to use social media to broadcast her loss, and in fact she worried about how participating in this way might add stress to her experience:

I think I texted like one or two people. I honestly told like one person, and I have groups of friends, so word goes around. [The response] was mostly [on] Facebook. I got some texts from my close friends and a few random ones, but more or less it was my close friends and like they would say, "Oh why didn't you tell me?," and I don't know, I didn't feel like [telling them] was my first priority. Because that was everyone's first priority—to pick up the phone. [My friends] also understand what type of person I am and how I respond to certain situations, so they were more understanding. I don't like to broadcast my problems on Facebook or any social media, I'll never be like, "Rest In Peace Daddy" like, "Oh, this is his birthday." I see that on other people's [pages] and I guess that's how they cope, but that's just not for me—because I just don't like when people, not so much pity, but look at me differently because of [the loss]. I don't find any type of "Oh I'm so sorry" comforting at all. Once one person sees that one thing—"Oh, I'm so sorry for your loss"—then other people ask, "Oh, who died?" and another, "Oh who's this for," . . . "Oh, what happened to her?" and then *everyone* knows about it.

Maureen and Rangani's reflections highlight how often the bereaved become witnesses to other people's perceptions of their grief. Many participants discussed the ways in which they often stood by while others offered condolences and discussed among themselves the impact of the loss. Many were hesitant to join the conversation and often tried to ignore blatant attempts by more distant acquaintances to "put on a show" related to offering social media–based condolences. Managing the spectacle and admonishing the inappropriateness of some displays was something that added stress to the grieving person and was something they chose to avoid.

Experiencing the loss via mobile media at times changed participants's relationship to their devices and to the ways in which they participated "online." The ambiguous nature of "how" to use technology in experiences related to death can sometimes cause interpersonal tension, and it can be used to prove to others the impact and authenticity of an experience, sometimes in shocking ways. As mentioned in a previous chapter, Laila's (18, Hispanic/Latina, US) father had urged his daughters to take a picture of their mother in the casket. Laila was very resistant to this but did it anyway. The picture that one of her sisters took was shared on social media, but Laila's photo remained on her phone. Laila did share it at times in unique ways:

[My friend] didn't believe [my mother died] and I guess I would take offense to that. I think someone joking about something as serious as [your mother dying] is very, very sad. For him to think [that] I would be taking advantage of [my mom dying]! Because it does happen (mothers dying)—if you are young or old or

whatever—it does! And I am like, "No! It's true!" And [he was]
like, "I can't believe it." I was like, "No, look!" And that is when
I would bring up the picture (of her in the casket). They would
be shocked that I would be so confident to show, it or they would
be shocked that it happened, because I guess it's not very common to hear that a seventeen-year-old lost their mom that young.
I was like, "You know, it does happen." Girls even lose their parents when they are younger, so I guess they are just surprised.

Even though Laila used the shock value of her digital photo to
convince others of her mother's death, the potential for social media
to make personal loss a public spectacle was something that many
US participants struggled with. The reality of loss, made readily
accessible through digital artifacts carried with the user in a digital
device, can be a source of comfort and validation at times.

Some participants resisted the use of social media for a variety
of reasons, often not related to the loss. William (18, Black, US)
explained in his interview, prior to being asked about the loss of his
friend Samuel, that he did not participate in social media because he
feared that it would be too much of a distraction in his life. When
talking about the loss of his friend and whether or not people had
posted about it on Facebook, William talked about how he had seen
Facebook posts about it. When asked how he saw these posts, he said
that while he did not have his own Facebook account, his brothers
did, and so he saw posts about his friend through one of his brother's
accounts. This was a fairly common experience, that access to social
media content was often shared, in person, between friends and
family.

Rather than accessing it on their own, at times the bereaved were
exposed to digital content, sometimes with reluctance, by others.
This highlights again the paradoxical nature of the ways in which use

of the mobile media can be comforting and can assist in the tasks of mourning, and yet, at the same time, expectations around mobile media use can be disorienting, stressful, and discomfiting. This echoes findings by Segerstad and Kasperowski in their study of Facebook as a support service for bereaved parents:

> The death of a child is an uncomfortable subject in most contemporary societies. This limits the exploration of experiences and possibilities for coping with grief. However, with the introduction of social media, this has changed. Theoretical perspectives on parental grief recognizing the importance of continued relational bonds with the lost child are used, together with the ontological assumption that social media enhance the dissolving of private/public and time/space. (2014, 1)

In their clinical theoretical understandings of bereavement, Segerstad and Kasperowski observe a five-stage process (denial, anger, bargaining, depression, and acceptance; cf. Kübler-Ross 2005) as part of a strategy for "resolving grief" or "letting go" (2014, 3). Alternatively, the dual process model (Stroebe, Schut, and Stroebe 2005) stresses developments of loss-oriented coping, restoration-oriented coping, and oscillation to understand how grief needs to be managed in maintaining continuing bonds with the deceased.

For Rosenblatt (1996) and Walter (1996), these Anglocentric models are problematic in that they try to resolve grief by breaking the bonds rather than by integrating them into the survivor's ongoing life. Parental grief is one of the hardest, most pathologized, and stigmatized processes in Western societies, as it involves contravening one of the tacit "natural" orders (Mitchell et al. 2012). In these studies, funerals are viewed as "closures" through which the bereaved's grief should be resolved (Mitchell et al. 2012).

However, other studies argue for the importance of continuing bonds through rituals. As Currier et al. (2015, 203) note, there is conflicting literature on the role of continuing bonds and its relationship to complicated grieving processes. We are reminded again of the significance of attachment as one of the primary paradigms for understanding grief and for understanding mobile-emotive co-presence. While attachment studies focus on attachment in and around people, objects and media also play an important role in attachment practices. Objects and media do not just mediate attachment, but can also be vehicles for attachment through the ascribing of symbolic values.

MOBILE MEDIA AS LINKING OBJECTS AND THE REALITY OF LOSS

Linking objects are discussed in the psychoanalytic literature as transitional objects, as a site for an intermediary experience whereby the holder of the object can feel as though they are not completely in the present reality, and that, through the object, they can still "hold on" to what has gone away (Mellos 2013). Mobile devices can serve exactly in this way as objects that link people to their past while they attempt to integrate themselves into the present. Through mobile media engagement, lost loved ones can seem as though they are always there—that in a moment's notice their presence can be conjured through the coveting of the ultimate treasured and transitional object—the mobile device.

As we have documented in the previous chapter through Sophie's attachment to John's phone, the mobile phone can serve as a linking object through which the continuation of bonds with the deceased can occur. The continuation of bonds usually occurs in three different ways: through physical, tangible representations of the deceased;

through linking objects; and through symbolic representation (Harper et al. 2011). The bereaved may spend time at gravesites or in possession of remains, but the continuation of bonds with the deceased usually relates to one's ability to carry around more portable linking objects and to attach symbolic representations of the deceased to those objects. The attachment the bereaved may feel toward artifacts (digital or otherwise) may indicate some denial of reality of the loss. However, in the ways that they are represented here, these objects appear to assist the bereaved in recognizing that the loss has occurred and in indicating the ways in which these losses have come to shape and define their identities. These objects also assist in the facilitation of ritual.

Linking objects can take on various forms. Again, traditionally, they are physical, tangible objects. Some participants demonstrated the ways in which digital artifacts have augmented, rather than replaced more traditional linking objects. The mobile device, while tangible, still allowed for the existence or connection to more symbolic and intangible artifacts. The tension between the meaningfulness of digital objects, as opposed to more tangible objects, was represented in the interviews. In fact, as we are establishing throughout this book, the poignancy of digital artifacts may do more to help honor the memory of the lost loved one than traditional (and tangible) memorial places such as gravesites or the personal effects that a loved one leaves behind. Bianca (19, Spanish/Hispanic, US) pointed this out:

> I feel like seeing her [through digital photos] as she was, is more [significant] than seeing a piece of land, you know, of her five feet under, or a plaque that says: "Rest in Peace, you will always be remembered."—I feel like that's not the image I want to have of her. The image I want to have of her is [of] me arriving at three or four o'clock in the afternoon and her already cooking what I am

going to be eating like five minutes into my day there, so that's the kind of picture I want to keep in my mind.

In reading this excerpt, one might think that Bianca was in denial of her grandmother's death, and that by not looking at the photos of the grave she could "pretend" that the loss did not occur. This was not the case for Bianca; her preference for photos of her grandmother alive served to strengthen her connection with her grandmother and ameliorated the fact that she was gone. Bianca was very aware that she would never again experience running into her grandmother's house after a long flight from America. However, that reality does not diminish the fact that she once did, and that her love for her grandmother endured. The digital picture of her grandmother in the kitchen did more to honor that memory than a picture of her gravesite. It is quite common, however, for the bereaved to deny the reality that the loss has occurred. Mobile devices can be tricky in this way, for as much as they can assist in the acceptance of the reality of the loss, they can also allow for the distorting and transcending of reality (see Chapter 7 for elaboration).

Because of mobile media, linking objects can now take on a hybrid fashion, becoming a mix between the material and immaterial. As Heather (22, White, Italian/Irish descent, US) described, whenever she tried on her grandmother's wedding ring that she kept at home, she would use her phone to take a picture of it, so she could use the photo later as a reminder of her grandmother. Her cousin mixed her grandmother's button collection with digital photos of her grandmother that she found online through social media to create mixed media mementos. Heather explained:

My grandma had this thing filled with buttons, so when we were little and went over we were like "Cool! You have this thing with all buttons" with really fancy [ones]. My cousin got them when [my grandma] passed, so she made us all a bracelet with them. She found pictures online [of our grandma] and put them on a little button, like in a little charm, and added it to [the bracelet she gave us].

Participants, like Heather, often discussed their linking objects with much affection and great attachment. Olivia (19, American with diverse ethnic background) participated in memorializing her great-grandmother online via Facebook and Instagram posts, but she also maintained tangible objects, namely a collection of necklace charms that she would wear every day to maintain and affirm her connection to her great-grandmother:

When I don't wear this necklace, I feel so weird. I think if I wear another necklace, I am like, "OK, she is not here today," and I have been wearing it since she passed. Like I haven't taken it off, like I sleep with it and everything, but if I go to a party and wear a fancier necklace, I'll take this off. I'll kiss it first, then I'll put it down. It's not like that she is NOT always on my mind, she is always somewhat there. It's just I am so busy that I don't have time to think of her. So I feel like wearing her, I know that she is there, like as if she was here.

The wearability of mobile devices may serve in a similar capacity to wearing a treasured necklace. Being able to connect to digital content served in a similar capacity as Olivia's necklace, in that these objects provided both a means to affirm the importance of the person in the bereaved person's life and a means to maintain a connection or bond to the deceased. In the ways that use of mobile media have been imagined in these interviews, and in the context of this entire book, for a majority of participants, mobile media was used as a tool to facilitate their grief process and to help them withstand the impact of a life forever changed by loss.

MOBILE MEDIA, LOSS, AND THE IMPACT ON IDENTITY

Frequent mobile media users may now rely more on mobile devices to assist them in understanding themselves and their role in others' lives. Our mobile devices may be tools that help us organize our social worlds, and they may reflect aspects of our emotional lives. They may also help us to understand which relationships are significant and which relationships define who we are. The use of mobile devices to access social networking sites has certainly increased the likelihood that most people have pre-existing social relationships, or some kind of tie (family, work, school), with the users they are connected to through these sites (boyd and Ellison 2007). Never before have people had the ability to elucidate, in so many ways, how they are connected to other people and how those connections affirm or detract from their sense of self.

The loss of a relationship with a significant other, whether it be through death or other forms of loss and separation, has the potential, at a minimum, to cause confusion and facilitate disruption in one's role and social identity. This disruption will occur with or without the integrated use of mobile media. However, the integration of social and mobile media into people's everyday life means that users can share their affect and emotions related to life experiences with a wide audience. In addition, Facebook status updates, in particular, were found to contain more emotionally charged language than the language in the reporting of experiences in more typical contexts (e.g., describing to someone two events that have happened in the day) (Lin, Tov, and Qiu 2014). It is important to note here that focusing on grief and loss brings to the surface the role that affect and emotion play in how we define relationships.

Many users in the United States engage with social media as a means to express their emotional investment in the world and their dependency on others to support their personal and professional goals. They may use this emotional labor (both within social media sites and within the digital artifacts stored on their mobile devices) to assist them in constructing their self-narrative. Profound losses can challenge our self-narrative, which Neimeyer, Klass, and Dennis define as

> an over-arching cognitive-affective-behavioral structure that organizes the "micro-narratives" of everyday life into a "macro-narrative" that consolidates our self-understanding, establishes our characteristic range of emotions and goals, and guides our performance on the stage of the social world. From this perspective, identity can be seen as a narrative achievement. That is, our sense of self is established through the stories that we tell about our lives, the stories that others tell about us, and the stories that we enact in their presence. (2014, 488–89)

The construction of self occurs through our ability to reflect on experiences that have occurred and in our attempts to explain them. We often generate self-narratives in dialogue with others. Responses to simple questions like "Why did you do that?" or "How did that make you feel?" require us to access some seemingly sensible coherent and congruent definitions of this thing we call our "selves." When a loss occurs, especially a loss that happens suddenly and unexpectedly, self-preservation tactics may shift into high gear and automatic attempts at regaining some sense of security and stability may require the bereaved to attempt to make sense of the loss that has occurred (Neimeyer, Klass, and Dennis 2014).

These sense-making processes can be done in dialogue with others, but often it is a deeply personal and private process. Being able to come up with some reason why the loss occurred often brings some relief to the bereaved and improves the individual's ability to cope with the loss. It allows for the bereaved to begin to acknowledge that the loss has occurred and the ways in which it has changed them. Traumatic loss shatters a person's assumptive world and can negatively impact one's belief in benevolence, the overall meaning of life, and one's own sense of value (Steffen and Coyle 2011). Part of the process of bereavement is to acknowledge how one has become defined by others, and what becomes evident are the ways in which people rely on their close ties to family and community to help them keep themselves together when their worlds "fall apart." In the next two sections, we discuss two ways in which the bereaved may engage in rituals using their mobile device to restore order to their sense of selves: mobile-emotive rituals of affirmation and of intensification. Through these rituals, one's social identity and role becomes salient. We identify these rituals as mobile-emotive for the ways in which individuals engage with mobile media to perform them.

MOBILE-EMOTIVE RITUALS OF AFFIRMATION

Rituals of affirmation mark the importance of the deceased in the loved one's life. Rituals of affirmation are those that are done to acknowledge the role that the deceased played in the life of the bereaved. These rituals are also centered on preserving the memory and acknowledging the contributions the deceased made while alive. This is a reflexive practice in that it is often defined both in ways in which the living would like to be remembered when it is their time to go, and in the expressed ways the deceased may have asked to be remembered. Rituals of affirmation allow for the bereaved to show appreciation toward the deceased for the contributions they have made to an individual's life (Doka 2002). These rituals center on the bereaved, in that they are an affirmation of their relationship to the deceased. These gestures of recognition contribute greatly to the post-mortem identities that get constructed for the deceased (Brubaker, Hayes, and Dourish 2013).

Postmortem identities (how individuals are known after death) are often based on self-concepts of the deceased that were accepted and acknowledged by others. These identities are broad-cast after death through recognition of the deceased's accomplishments and their relationships with others. In death, survivors must decide which aspects of the deceased's identity should be preserved and which aspects should be forgotten. Unruh (1983) calls this process "strategies of identity preservation." The process of preserving a person's identity after death usually begins with sharing memories and openly acknowledging the role that the person played in the lives of the bereaved. Artifacts from the deceased, such as treasured photos or meaningful objects, may be collected and displayed as evidence to support these claims (Unruh 1983). However, unlike any other time in history, the ways in which people use and access social and mobile media can have undue influence on this process.

As mentioned previously, it is important to remember that, despite whatever is being broadcast in the quasi-public space of social networking sites, personal mobile devices allow for the bereaved to preserve their own private rituals of affirmation. These mobile-emotive rituals often lead to the symbolic representations of relationships through the use of digital artifacts, such as digital photos and other media. Many participants talked about using photos as their background (wallpaper) photos, or just storing photos on their phones as reminders of the significant role that their loved one played in their life. What was also interesting was the fact that some participants digitized older forms of media just so they could access it on their mobile devices. Participant Kaltrina (19, Muslim/Albanian, US) explained how this functioned in relation to the loss of her grandfather:

> On my other phone, I had pictures, I had [pictures of pictures], the actual photo, that I took a picture of with [my] camera [phone]. Only a few weeks after one of my grandfathers died, and I was looking at pictures [from a box of photos] and I saw one of us: of me and my grandfather and my brothers. So I took [a picture of that with the camera phone]. I set that as my wallpaper. It would actually make me feel happy because I didn't think of how he died but I thought of the good times we had, and I remembered all the fun stuff. [I look at it] when I'm feeling upset about something—I'll look at it because it makes me happy.

Kaltrina described how the picture was just for her, as a reminder to her of who her grandfather was and the role that he played in her life. This was not unlike how Bianca used her picture of her grandmother in the kitchen. One cannot deny that this was an attempt to continue their bonds with their grandparents, as well as a means to affirm how significant their grandparents were in their lives. Using a special photo as wallpaper on her phone meant Kaltrina could share the picture with others when asked, but choosing it as her wallpaper was a personal decision and indicative of the ritualistic aspect of the use of digital media to affirm her relationship as a means of coping with grief. As mentioned previously, digital content does not replace more tangible artifacts, but the ability to have both, and to have both forms of media interact with each other, was something that Heather explained helped her stay connected to her grandmother and to affirm the important place she had in Heather's life:

> I found pictures that I have with her that were taken from a camera, put online, and I transferred them to my phone because I want to have them. I have gone out of my way to take other pictures to put them on my phone so that I can always have them with me. So if I am like, "Oh I want to look," I just . . . sometimes [they] are a reminder that I should go more to the cemetery. I just like to look at them [on my phone] to be reminded of good times. So I can [be like], "Oh look!" and scroll through and look at them on my phone, but then if I go home I can see a new one [in the photo albums], and I can keep them separate.

Heather's archiving of digital and material artifacts was important to her. It took on a ritualistic flair and it was something that she did more for herself, to affirm her relationship and identity, but it was also something that she readily shared with others through their shared familial connection to her grandmother.

Posts to social media can also be interpreted as rituals of affirmation. Many participants noted how they would claim their lost loved ones via social media as a means of affirming the relationship and the significant role that the deceased played in their lives. Sometimes these posts would take on a conversational tone as a device for communicating the nature of the relationship, and in this way they served a dual purpose, being both an attempt to continue one's bond with the deceased and a way to broadcast to others the significance of the relationship and the significance of the loss. These personal and individual means of memorializing relationships become a source of comfort and affirmation to the bereaved. Olivia explained this:

Um, I wrote it [an RIP post to her grandma] just to write it, but people did comment, which I didn't think they would. I mean obviously my family commented. I know my family was like, "I know Olivia, we miss her so much," in that we were all getting through it together. I do it just to honor [my grandma], I mean it's not like she [is going to] pull up Facebook and read it. But I feel like, I don't know, I feel like it's just like a nice thing to do. It is basically in honor of her, especially since she was so important. It is definitely not for the attention! But it is like a public affection kind of thing. It is like a memorial but on Facebook. Like a roadside memorial, Facebook has nothing to do with my great-grandma, but I think it's comforting to just put it out there.

As Olivia's comments indicate, rituals of affirmations often reveal not only the significance of the individual to the bereaved, but also the connections that the deceased had to others. When a member of a group is lost, the stability of that group is threatened, and as such, those experiencing the loss will reach out to others as a means to cushion the impact of the loss. This can be done quite easily through the use of mobile media. In the next section, we highlight mobile-emotive rituals of intensification as a means through which rituals of affirmation can be expanded to include a deeper sense of connectedness among family and community.

MOBILE-EMOTIVE RITUALS OF INTENSIFICATION

Mobile-emotive rituals of intensification are rituals that strengthen connection among group members and reinforce their common identity (Wheeler-Roy and Amyot 2004). Despite an effort to affirm the significance of the deceased in one's life, any loss can pose some threat to an individual's ability to identify with their relational groups. Losses can cause disruptions in routines and expectations, and they can result in a shifting of roles within familial and communal groups (Amore and Scarciotta 2011). Many traditional rituals around death are about bringing family and community together to surround the mourners with support, and about providing close ties to those who can be relied upon to offer assistance in maintaining the bereaved's most basic needs.

For those who have more diasporic identities or who may have been separated from their cultures of origin or families, this separation can be particularly painful during times of grief and loss. While mobile technology provides a link between those who have experienced this kind of loss through the ability to transgress geographic distance, other distances are amplified. Much of the work around diasporas and mobile technologies highlights ambiguities and paradoxes (McKay 2012). Thanks to webcam services like FaceTime and Skype, loved ones can be almost instantly connected with their families and friends abroad. More than just a voice call, people can see what is occurring, and so they are able to participate in grief rituals that are meant to intensify the connection between those that share a common identity. Sometimes the webcam—with its overemphasis on the visual, and often with temporal pauses and interruptions—can further highlight the distance. However, for many of our US participants, like Kaltrina, the webcam facilitated connections with their loved ones abroad:

[My mom] got a call from her sister, my aunt in Austria, which found out from the family. After that we talked on video chat on MSN (Microsoft Network) to everyone in Albania and Austria. I felt really bad because my mom couldn't go to the funeral because she had to work. But we had a lot of people come to help us because we still have some family here, but most of our family is over there [and] when they had the time to video chat, we video chatted but we couldn't really video chat the whole time. They tried to reassure [my mom], to try to make her feel better—I think it did help her to have them there [via video chat].

The ability to video chat can thus help ameliorate the pain of the geographical distance between loved ones when delivering the news of a loved one's passing and when not being able to attend funeral services in person. Participants also discussed the ways in which social media was used to participate in rituals that helped to bring the family closer together as the result of the loss. This was often done through the sharing of pictures, as alluded to in Laila's sister sharing pictures of her mother's funeral. Relatives sent Bianca a picture of her grandmother's grave, since she was not able to travel to attend the funeral. Documentary evidence of funereal rites and burials was sent to participants whose loved one's died abroad. This was done as a means of reassurance that the loss or the geographical distance did not sever their connections and ties to their social, cultural, and familial groups.

People use social and mobile media to create mobile-emotive rituals of intensification that would not exist without the help of social media. In fact, these rituals may act as a motivation to participate in social media. As mentioned previously, Chantal (19, Jamaican, US) was reluctant to use any technology after her boyfriend's murder, but her friends convinced her to create her own Facebook page so that she could access a memorial group page that was created to honor her boyfriend. Chantal stated clearly that if there was no memorial page and group, she would not be on Facebook:

Yeah that's why I made a Facebook, 'cause my friend told me, "Oh well, they have a group page, and you should like make a Facebook because everyone is looking for you!" [They were saying] "How come she doesn't have a Facebook page?" and "I think she should create one." So I made a Facebook and then they sent me a request [to join the group].

Chantal discussed how she came onto Facebook for the sole purpose of intensifying her connection to those who knew her boyfriend. As we have demonstrated, online memorial pages are used to create links and more enduring ties between those who knew the deceased (Brubaker, Hayes, and Dourish 2013). These connections would be weaker and perhaps nonexistent without the assistance of social and mobile media. Heather's family had experienced multiple losses within a short period. Like John's family in the previous chapter, Heather's cousin created a group on Facebook where their family could stay in touch and share memories of their lost loved ones. The sharing of digital content appeared to intensify their connections with each other. As Heather explained,

> We have a group chat that my cousin made and we use that a lot to post things. It is a page; a closed group. Every member of my family is in it, we don't do (paper) invitations anymore for small events, we just do it all online. I think it did help keep us a little bit closer. If anyone has a feeling or anything we can just put it there, and it is out for everyone. I think it was a little bit of a wake-up call that now my parents and our aunts and uncles are now the elders of the family, I think that is kind of like, "Oh shit." Like this is it. I think it definitely helped to try to be like, "We have to really keep it together," we are all very close, but as we get older we all tend to separate, and so we have to keep it close, so it's definitely a wake-up call.

As Heather stated, losses in families can serve as a "wake-up" call to the impermanence of life. Losses also force shifts in roles and identities within familial and cultural groups. The US participants narrated the ways in which the shifts in the family structure caused by loss were reflected in expressions on social media. Again, social media was also used to strengthen and intensify the ties between those impacted by the loss.

CONCLUSION: MOBILE-EMOTIVE RITUALS AS EXTENSIONS OF TRADITION AND OF SELF

Mobile-emotive rituals of affirmation and intensification serve as a means to honor the contribution that the deceased made to the lives they were connected to. It was important to many participants that they engaged in mobile-emotive rituals that emphasized that their loved ones were not forgotten. It was also affirming when participants recognized that others were also engaged in the activity of remembering the lost loved one. Gestures made via mobile media by friends and family were seen to hold some value to the bereaved. It was seen as a "nice" gesture to ensure that the loss was acknowledged in some way. For most, participating in mobile-mediated rituals of affirmation and intensification was seen as doing something "good" for the dead.

Rituals of affirmation and intensification appear inherent in many of the more typical memorializing activities, like the construction of the roadside memorial or the renaming of a street to honor the deceased. Memorials, in general, serve as a means to gain some ability to perpetuate the ties people still have with each other despite the loss. Social and mobile media have the potential to make it very easy to perform these kinds of rituals. The ease with which these mobile-emotive rituals can be enacted means that these activities can continue indefinitely and may be more enduring than a signpost placed on the side of the road. Mobile devices also make it easier to maintain ties with those who knew the deceased. Social media's ability to generate social networks and social media groups can work to help define those connections.

The relationship that the bereaved participants have with their technology was in some ways changed after a loss. This change could be reflective of the ways in which an individual's social and emotional worlds were disrupted by loss. Rituals of affirmation and intensification highlight the ways in which loss allows the user to extend the typical and ordinary use of technology to include extraordinary ways of continuing a sense of communication with the deceased. In the next chapter we grapple with mobile-emotive rituals of transition and letting go, and elaborate on the ways that mobile media now challege traditional grief trajectories.

Transition and Letting Go

We were on the phone a lot, when I wasn't with her—when she was still able [to]—when she was coherent—we were on the phone a lot. That's why I can't delete her number on my phone. I have her cell phone, and her house number [in my phone], and I can't get rid of it. [Another friend I work with] deleted her number. She said, "I had to, it hurt," and I said, "I can't and I haven't," and I saw that [woman] recently and I showed her [that I still have the number in my phone], and she's was like, "You're crazy." But it's weird to me. I feel like it's like deleting her from my life. I don't know. I know that's stupid but that's how I feel; and she laughed at me and so I'm like, alright [laughs]. (Gabrielle, 41, Greek/American, US)

Gabrielle's experience is one that other US participants shared. Many of them felt pressure from other people to delete their digital ties to their lost loved ones. Deleting phone numbers and texts was viewed as "healthy" and as a necessary part of "letting go." "Helpful friends" would often have a hand in pushing the heartbroken to "get over" their loss by deleting digital content. The purging of mobile media has come to represent a psychological distancing from emotion-triggering material. This psychological distancing reduces the emotional intensity of the digital content.

As noted earlier, until very recently, the most accepted models of bereavement in Western psychology focused on a grieving arc that would end with the bereaved "letting go" of the deceased and moving on with their lives. Any continuing bond with the deceased would be seen as a symptom of a more complicated and pathological form of grieving (Klass, Silverman, and Nickman 1996). This focus began within the field of psychology in 1917, when Sigmund Freud published his essay "Mourning and Melancholia." In the essay, Freud normalized the grief response and called it *Trauer*, a German word that does not have a direct English translation. The translator, in a footnote, remarked, "the German *Trauer*, like the English "mourning," can mean both the effect of grief and its outward manifestation. Throughout the paper, the word has been rendered as 'mourning'" (Freud 1917, 243). Named as such, mourning came to represent not just the state or the reality that the loss had occurred, but also the emotions of grief and sorrow that followed. Freud then established a set of expectations that normalized mourning. Successful completion of the mourning task would result in a "letting go" based on a kind of logical, yet self-protective, realization of the loss.

Freud wrote about the bereaved person's unconscious attachment to the lost "object" as reflected in the rumination of memories related to the deceased and the pain resulting from the failed expectation that occurs in situations where the deceased, in the past, would be present, but is no longer. Every time the lost object is not there, not present, not where it "should" be, every time the bereaved person is reminded of the deceased or intentionally reflects on memories of the deceased, the reality of the loss is brought into closer view. This recognition then stimulates a kind of anxiety in the living person.

By acknowledging the reality of death, the living person feels threatened by it, and out of self-preservation needs to "sever its attachment to the thing that has been abolished" (Freud 1917, 255). This letting go was seen as a survival tactic, because the living fear the reality of their own death. The severing of ties with the lost object was viewed as the only way to protect oneself from death anxiety and the more pathological form of grief called "melancholia." Freud posited that people do not engage the process of letting go willingly; it is instead a painful but necessary process that takes a long time to complete.

Freud then provided a prescription to psychotherapists and supportive others: encourage the bereaved in the process of letting go. The process of letting go was ultimately seen as a step toward surviving the loss and reducing its emotional and physical pain. This ability to "let go," especially of some emotionally powerful digital content, may feel necessary to allow for the integration of the loss to occur in the lives of those left behind. Many of the participants narrated the intense connection they had to digital linking objects related to the loss, as described in previous chapters. These linking objects affirmed the relationship that the bereaved had with their lost loved ones. These objects came to represent both physical and virtual remnants and reminders of the person. These linking objects were also the means through which some participants were able to reanimate aspects of their lost loved ones. Resistance to "letting go" of digital content could be related to the bereaved person's resistance to adjusting to a life without the deceased, and also a resistance to severing the ties with their loved ones.

In this chapter, we explore some of the ways in which mobile media and mobile-emotive rituals break these traditional notions of grief and the need to "let go." Here again, we see the specific affordances mobile media create in the continuation of bonds. As in previous chapters, we are not positioning ourselves within the psychological debate of whether or not people *should* let go or sever ties with the deceased or with treasured objects. Rather, we have taken the position that traditional psychological notions of the grieving process do not include more narrative approaches toward understanding the meaning-making processes related to grief. We have demonstrated the powerful ways that mobile media can assist in continuing bonds with lost loved ones. What we are focusing on in this chapter are the ways in which mobile media users, especially in the United States, use mobile-emotive rituals in the regulation of emotional intensity. This need to regulate emotional intensity may arise from pressure to conform to traditional grief trajectories of "letting go." In this, we investigate how US participants described their motivations behind whether or not they deleted digital content, and how, for some of these participants, changes made to content or devices indicated a mobile-emotive transition in their grief process.

According to Wheeler-Roy and Amyot (2004), rituals of transition indicate a change in the grief response. Most bereaved people in the West encounter mourning as a process, as something to "get through" or "get over." Those that surround or companion the bereaved in these contexts are often looking for indicators that the bereaved are moving in some direction toward resilience, toward restoration. Rituals of transition often involve some degree of anxiety, because the social pressure to conform to others' expectations may not be easy to manage alongside the bereaved person's attempt to adjust to a new understanding of their world. Grief inevitably changes everything. Rituals of transition are about putting the pieces of one's life back together and about narrating one's journey in grief. These rituals are about adaptation. They are about survival. The anxiety around and resistance to these rituals can be ameliorated when participation in the rituals is motivated by the bereaved themselves (Doka 2002). These rituals can be viewed as a necessary tool in grappling with the pain of grief and with the unfinished business that loss leaves behind.

Mobile devices are often quite proficient in reminding us of all the business left unfinished. This extends to mourning contexts in that digital content has the potential to emphasize the loose ends of loss. Mobile-emotive rituals of transition can encompass the ways in which the bereaved grapple with this and the ways in which digital specters must be dealt with, just as with any other belongings of the deceased.

In this chapter, we will first grapple with the ways in which mediated communication via mobile devices can be used to regulate emotion. We discuss the role of the archive in the mourning process as a means through which we can better understand the difficulty of managing the digital remains that people leave behind. We then explore how some people cultivate mobile-emotive rituals of transition and the ways in which mobile media use can indicate changes in a person's grief response. Some mourners may consider the severing of ties with the deceased as part of their transition. We will demonstrate how the severance of ties becomes increasingly complicated because of the integration of mobile devices into our everyday lives. Ultimately, mobile-emotive rituals of transition are about the ways in which adjusting to a "new normal" becomes complicated by mobile media's tendency to underscore users' habits and routines, which then may lead to painful reminders of the loss and challenge any attempt at "letting go."

THE POWER OF MOBILE-EMOTIVE ARCHIVES AND THE DECOMPOSITION/DELETION OF DIGITAL ARTIFACTS

Mobile media can take both material and immaterial forms in the mourning processes of "letting go." In dealing with both the material and digital possessions of the deceased, the bereaved may integrate the use of mobile media into how they deal with what is retained and what is disposed of. The process of the dispersal of possessions may not happen right away. In fact, many people resist changing anything about their worlds as a means of maintaining some transitory space between the reality of loss and the unreality of grief. As mentioned previously in this book, controlling the use of objects serves as a means to maintain connections to the deceased. Deciding how to engage in letting go of objects related to the deceased is both an individual and complex process. US participant Maureen (18, White) hinted at how holding on to both material and immaterial possessions functioned as a way to hold on to her deceased father:

> His desk is still where it always was and I like things like that—that certain things are still the way they used to be and this [digital photo] is just . . . instead of him being there [at his desk]—he is just there [Maureen points to phone].

Maureen's determination to hold on to both the desk and the digital photos emphasized her desire to keep her father's presence firmly in her life. Multiple times throughout the US interviews, it was remarkable to witness the ways in which the storing and archiving capability of the mobile device took precedence over its communication functionality. In this, the phone's ability to archive the past took on emotional and psychological significance. It may be important here to discuss the role that archives play in our remembering (and forgetting) of the past, as an emotional experience, for they work to

> remind us; by virtue of their material existence they bring the past to mind. . . . If they function as a kind of external and material memory—as both "personal" memory for personal archives and "social" or 'collective' memory for national repositories—then any degradation or dissolution in the archives must be understood as a kind of forgetting. (Cooke and Reichelt-Brushett 2015, 10–11)

Any reluctance to delete archived digital content may carry with it a fear of forgetting, as well as a sense of disrespect due to the virtual disappearance of the lost loved one (Vincent 2010). Maintaining a sense of presence of the deceased through the archiving of digital content may be, on some level, a refusal to let go of the dead and a rejection of the finality of death. Yet despite its role in possibly encouraging denial, this content also may assist the bereaved in coming to terms with the reality of the loss (Bennett and Bennett 2000). In addition to the digital content stored on an individual's phone, digital archives can be created and maintained, as well as shared by others, through social media. Reviewing shared remembrances and treasured photos via social media usually happens upon hearing the news of a loved one's death, especially if they had any social media presence, or if their loved ones did. Many US participants discussed coveting digital artifacts for their ability to provide a private "space" in which to grieve. The preference for privacy around the grieving process and the means through which people could generate intimate spaces within the mobile-emotive archive stored on the device, set grieving via mobile media apart from other kinds of mediated online grief. Bianca talked about how much she coveted her digital photo archive:

> I screen-shotted [sic] all of them to my phone (She had viewed the pictures first on her brother's laptop). I cropped it out so it will only be her [in the] picture, I showed it to my mom, I showed it to everyone. [The pictures on my phone] mean a lot—I back up the pictures, I save them to the computer. I save them on my laptop. I probably have them saved in three different portable devices. My brother has them saved on his phone. My father, my mom, everyone has them saved.

Participants, like Bianca (19, Spanish/Hispanic, US), often mentioned how meaningful and important digital archives were, and that at times they were seen as having the potential to be more enduring and longer-lasting than more tangible physical objects. The ability to digitize "real photos" meant that they would never be lost or destroyed. Users also felt as though they had more control over these objects. Rituals around archiving these artifacts again reified their sacredness. Many US participants characterized their mobile devices as portable memory boxes. The co-constructed nature of the narrative and graphic content archived on the digital device allows for the owner of the material to manipulate and control it. As a result, the digital specters left behind can never be an exact replica of the deceased, and the degeneration and separation from such content could be analogous to another form of the decomposition of the corpse. Decomposition, in its many forms, may frame letting go of the deceased as a "natural conclusion" to the grieving process.

Participants mentioned how letting go was expected to be part of the grieving process, especially when their access was diminished by a loss of immediate connection to emotionally charged archives via their mobile device. Losing access to stored content could, in essence, speed up the letting go process. As Laila (18, Hispanic/Latina, US) explained,

[When I switched phones] I did lose [my mother's] voicemails. Because this is a new phone, it is not like they are going to transfer it over. But I still have that phone, I am able to not activate it but turn it on, and I still have videos on that phone and pictures and stuff like that so I am able to see it. It was hard [to lose the voicemails]. I remember I was kind of mad [at the phone company]. I was like, "Is there any way that you could transfer my voicemails over?" And they were like, "No." And then I was like, "Why? What if they are important?" They were like. "We're sorry." And then I was like, "Alright." Because I didn't want to start a problem about it. Because I was like, you know, it's fine— even though I can't access it on this phone I can still hear it on my old phone. I just couldn't access them on [my current phone].

(*Interviewer: So you didn't lose them completely?*) No, but [the old phone is] not always with me. Because I am not going to carry two phones with me, that's just too much.

As Laila described, the bereaved often do not have a choice as to whether they separate from meaningful digital archives, because sometimes the purging of content happens when the user must change devices. The disposable nature of some devices (e.g., being replaced by newer technology; switching providers; phones breaking, getting stolen, or being given away; etc.) may make them less reliable than older forms of archiving like saving printed pictures in photo albums. When asked if she transferred her pictures from her old phone to her new iPhone, Olivia (19, American, with diverse ethnic background, US) replied,

No, I don't think they could. I don't think they were able to, I don't know what the thing was. Because at the time I was just so excited to get an iPhone, I didn't even care [laughs]. I just like dropped the old phone on the side of the road [laughing hard]. No, I still knew I was going to have [the old phone] anyway. Because I am sure there is a way . . . How do you transfer? I am sure there is a way, but I was like, "Yes! I am getting an iPhone! BYE!" [laughs]. It's like, "Bye, old memories!" Not really, but it's kind of, and I still have [the old phone]. It's not like I look at it all the time, but I still have it if I am going to.

Olivia was amused by how the prospect of gaining a new device overshadowed her concern about replacing the phone that contained the treasured digital artifacts related to her great-grandmother. She was reassured that even with the switching of phones, retaining her old phone meant she could still access the content on it. For both Olivia and Laila, their old devices became like time capsules that they could revisit whenever they wanted to. The seeming loss of access to content through the switching of mobile services was ameliorated by the fact that stored digital content did not require access to the network. Based on how strong the ties were to digital archives, it is important to mention here that more favorable psychological outcomes result from the bereaved person having control over whether or not digital content is deleted. Losing digital linking objects can trigger a loss all over again. There is something about holding onto the digital content that feels grounding and solidifying, but when the loss of that content is out of their control, it can be traumatic. US participants discussed how painful it was to adjust to changes in mobile-mediated communication with loved ones and how the deletion of digital content made it worse. As Carly (18, White, US) explained in discussing the fallout from her romantic breakup,

> I didn't save his number on my phone! I deleted his number. So I wouldn't be tempted to text him or call him. I deleted our pictures and our conversations and everything. I actually remember being next to my best friend and she was like forcing me to delete them; I didn't want to delete them, but she was telling me that if I don't delete them that it would torture me and I would keep looking at them. So I deleted it. She watched me do it. She made sure I did it.

Carly described how, through her friend's urging, she was able to delete the digital traces of her ex-boyfriend on her phone. She acknowledged that by holding on to that content she was continuing her connection to him. Both she and her friend viewed this purging of digital content as something painful but still a necessary part of the breakup. Carly continued,

> Oh it was horrible, I regretted it—now it's, whatever—but at the time I regretted it. I didn't really want to delete them because

I just didn't want him to be gone but I knew that he had to be. I just really didn't want to. (*Interviewer: If you had a friend going through this, would you give her the same advice to delete everything?*) I would! Because if they are out of sight, they are out of mind—it's a lot easier to forget about them if they are not appearing in everywhere you look and in every time you open your phone you see them. Even though you will eventually look them up on a social media site, they just are not always there.

Carly understood the deleting of digital content as a means through which she could achieve closure and separation from her ex-boyfriend. She knew it was a necessary step related to modern-day romance that the digital remnants of relationships have the potential to pop up and serve as constant reminders that what once was a source of pleasure is now only painful. The deletion of concrete digital evidence does not preclude, as Carly pointed out, covert attempts at maintaining a bond—secretly and beyond the awareness of others—through social media monitoring. We also discovered that some participants used mobile media to purge their emotions. US participant Aminah (18, Syrian/Arabic) described how she used the Notepad app on her phone as a "place" where she could purge her emotions and achieve some psychological distance from the emotional intensity of her loss:

Sometimes, even if I can't talk to anyone, I know this sounds crazy, but I'll just go and I'll just type how I feel, and just let it all out, and it helps. [I type it out to myself] in my Notepad [app]. It's such a release. It makes me feel better, yeah, like I'm getting something off my chest, if I can't send it, I'll just leave it and it does help. It's my way of getting through it.

Aminah chose to dump her feelings into her Notepad app as a means of regulating the emotional intensity of her experience. It appears that mobile-emotive rituals can work to ameliorate anything that complicates the grief process. Digital archives can be used to assist in resolving the typical roadblocks that lead to disenfranchised or complicated grief. In the next section, we will demonstrate how mobile media users engage their ability to regulate their emotions through their mobile media as a means to facilitate giving up mobile-emotive "ghosts" and the severance of ties.

GIVING UP MOBILE-EMOTIVE GHOSTS AND THE SEVERING OF TIES

The open-channel nature of mobile technology—to be discussed in further detail in Chapter 7—complicates closure, letting go, or moving on. The open-endedness of mobile media may be the cause for friends of some participants to intervene in order to ensure that the severing of ties or attempts at closure took place via the deleting of phone numbers, past text messages, photos, and so on. This severance of ties often included blocking others from social media accounts (as in the case of romantic breakups) or the taking down of social media pages (as in the case of death). US participant Carly explained the whole blocking procedure and the motivation of her ex-boyfriend to block her:

> He blocked me on Facebook [right after the breakup conversation] so I couldn't see him or anything. It is not that I couldn't be friends with him, it's that if he wrote on something, if we had a mutual friend and he commented on it, I couldn't see his comment, so it was like he wasn't even existing any more. And he blocked me on Instagram as well. I could still see his Instagram, but I couldn't see his pictures.

The methodical way in which Carly described how her ex-boyfriend chose to go about blocking her on social media took on a tone of acquiescence and acceptance. However, her tone was mainly related to the fact that she was forced to accept it because he did it. Even though she felt compelled to accept it, there was a part of her that still longed for staying connected with him via social media. Carly explained:

> (*Interviewer: How did it make you feel to experience the blocking part?*) It was really like you lost him more because you have no connection to him anymore, and I don't speak to him. It was just like he's gone. He told me that he blocked me for my own good because he knew that I would be constantly looking him up and look at what he was doing, and see his pictures. So he said, "I'm going to block you," because he said that he knew that I would look him up. It made sense, but the whole conversation was weird—I had no idea that that was going to happen.

It was interesting to note that Carly and her ex-boyfriend both discussed what was to happen to their social media connection after the breakup. Carly's ex-boyfriend decided that it would be best for them to not have any contact via social media because that was what would be best for Carly. Carly's ex-boyfriend's perspective was shared by other participants. Dwelling on the past through the coveting of digital content and social media connection was sometimes interpreted as being psychologically torturous or masochistic. A person's sense of well-being was viewed as being compromised by having ready access to mobile media related to a loss and by revisiting that material over and over again. Some participants narrated how a sense of purging was what was required to "get over" the loss. This was usually combined with the strategy of not thinking about and not talking about the loss. This strategy usually required avoiding content related to the loss via mobile communication and social media along with avoiding any attempts by others to discuss the loss. US participant David (18, Hispanic) adopted the "don't think/don't talk about it" strategy for processing his grief:

> (*Interviewer: What were some of the things you found helped you cope with the loss immediately after it happened?*) Honestly, I tried not to think about it. Honestly, it is pretty vague to me. I think somebody messaged me: "Oh why aren't you texting me back?" I would read it and it would tell them that [I] read it, and they said, "Why are you reading my text messages and not responding?" I don't really put my business out there—I am very private.

David avoided contact with others related to his loss because he felt the pressure to be stoic and to remain in control of his emotions. He believed that his demeanor assisted his family in being able to express their emotions without fear of their whole world falling apart. David did not feel as though it served any purpose to dwell on the loss of his close family friend. By maintaining some psychological distance from it, he felt confident in his emotional strength, his ability to "move on," and his resistance to feeling any continued bond with his dearly departed friend. He was not comfortable with ruminating over memories or photos (despite him creating a digital slideshow for the funeral that he saved on his computer and shared with extended family), and was uneasy at the suggestion that he might revisit and review that slideshow out of the context of the funeral or family gathering.

Some people felt unease with maintaining digital remains of lost connections with others on their phones because it felt like a haunting. At times the unanticipated nature of the lost loved one "popping up" on their phone was viewed as unsettling. Participants experienced this in losses related to death, whereby they experienced being afraid of the phone and sometimes worried that their loved one's spirit might be trapped in their device. Thus, deleting digital content became much like purging a ghost. Portia (18, African American, US) spoke of this:

> I was looking through my phone, and I saw the pictures [of Lucy, who died] and I was like, you know what, she is gone. It was a month or two later. It is time to delete it and let it go. So I was just deleting them. Bit by bit and saying goodbye [to her] at the same time. I felt relieved, I felt calm, I felt like I was holding on to something—the pictures kind of took space. So I just let go of the pictures.

In this description, Portia related the deleting of the digital photos of Lucy from her phone as a mobile-emotive ritual aimed at freeing up some psychological space. At first, this appeared to have all the markers of a mobile-emotive ritual of transition. After being questioned further, however, the true motivation for her deletion ritual revealed itself:

> I don't like to go to funerals or watch scary movies with ghosts or something, I avoid those kinds of things. Well [laughs], some of [Lucy's] pictures [were like] if you go into a museum and some pictures if you walk past, you feel like the eyes are watching you? That's how it was with that one, so I just deleted it quickly. (*Interviewer: So does the phone have the potential to be haunted?*) It could. It could. In my mind, say I had her picture here, I would think that she would go through the phone, like her spirit would be in the phone. Every time I [turned] on the phone her picture would show up out of nowhere. That would be kind of scary. That is why I had to get rid of them, so that won't happen.

Portia reported that the pictures of Lucy became creepy after her death. Portia felt as though they were "alive" in her phone, and she feared Lucy's spirit would become trapped in her phone. Features of the phone itself contributed to this experience. On her Galaxy handset, all of her photos were stored in a pile on her home screen. Whenever she opened her phone, she would see a photo of Lucy. The eyes in all of these photos disturbed her until she decided to delete all twelve photos ritualistically. To keep the photos would risk being haunted by them.

In deleting the pictures, Portia felt as though her phone no longer trapped Lucy's spirit. In a way, removing the photos released Portia from her grief as well. She and her mother both felt that it was "unhealthy" to hold on to the photos or to dwell on the past. Some participants also reported this as a part of their experience—that the digital content had the potential to "trap" people (not necessarily spirits) in the emotionality of the loss, and that it seemed better to let go and move on.

For others, the lingering aspects of grief and sorrow were facilitated through the mobile-emotive aspects of mourning. Melancholia is characterized as a pathological devotion to the lost object, a refusal to let go, a refusal to rejoin the living (Hagenmaier 2009). Mobile media can provide a means through which melancholia and longing can be sustained and kept secret. It can be a constant digital overlay in the daily life of the bereaved person. The open-channel nature of mobile communication means that communication never truly ends, especially in something like a romantic breakup; the longing for the possibility of reconnection is always there. The connection may be severed, but never completely broken, as long as one party has the means to contact the other. The personal nature of the mobile device, found in the US context, can keep that longing for reconnection private and yet viable. In essence, the door is never closed. Jackie (22, American/Italian-Greek descent, US) explained this in response to her holding on to all the text messages exchanged between her and her ex-boyfriend:

> It definitely makes it worse. I can always just go on my phone and just look at it. If it wasn't there, I would feel better because then I would know that I can't go in my phone and look at what we said, but I feel it makes it worse, like I tried to delete him but I can't. . . . I don't delete it though. All the pictures of my ex are all the way at the top; I won't be able to see it unless I want to see it, unless I scroll up. Like some nights, I am not going to lie, I always look through everything before I go to sleep. But some nights I just want to get over him already and it's just annoying. It is harder, like I walk out of my house and I see his house.

The melancholic nature of this kind of attachment to digital content could be seen as a less productive result of the grieving process. Yet does melancholia and longing for connection need to be patholo- gized? In reconceiving melancholia, one could view it as a passionate space of potentiality:

> This potential space, phantasmic alternative reality, allows for an engagement with loss that is lively, imaginative, and active, far from stable and dead. . . . This space is not a pathological hallucination or regressive escape from responsibility as Freud might suggest, but rather . . . a hopeful place for imagining alter- native ties between past and present, loss and what remains. (Hagenmaier 2009, 161)

US participants discussed the ways in which they used their grief to reimagine aspects of themselves and to be released, in some way, from the limitations of other people's definitions of their relationships with lost loved ones. Despite the belief that the lost object somehow threatens the living, in death the mobile-emotive essences of what remains were used by participants to bolster their connection to the living. The struggle between maintaining a connection to what has been lost and recognizing when to let go and what is important to let go of is the essence of grief work. As mentioned in the beginning of this chapter, grief work models have dominated the study of mourning within Western psychology (Russac, Steighner, and Canto 2002). The idea of working through loss and arriving at some destination of recovery still occupies the mind of most mourners in the West. In the next section, we discuss how mobile-emotive rituals of transition assist the bereaved in recognizing shifts within their grieving process.

MOBILE-EMOTIVE RITUALS OF TRANSITION

Mobile-emotive rituals of transition highlight the ways in which mobile media users understand how changes in their engagement with mobile technology could be a part of how their grieving process has changed. Mobile-emotive rituals of transition were noted in US participants' recognition of how the emotional intensity of their first posts changed over time as compared to later posts. Olivia remarked that she noticed that in the three years since her great-grandmother had passed, the intensity of her grief had subsided. She mentioned how time was a factor that was helping her cope with her loss. In discussing the memorial posts she had made to honor her great-grandmother, Olivia noted how the amount of text within each post had decreased over time. For Olivia, this meant that the intensity of her grief had shifted as well:

> Um, [the anniversary memorial posts are] usually kind of like the same thing—just the year changes . . . pretty much I am kind of like, "RIP, can't believe it's been how many years since you are gone,

you were an amazing woman—we miss you so much." Things like that. But I think it's like, I don't want to say, dying down, but it's not as the first time, when she first passed—like it will go from a novel, to a paragraph, to a sentence, to like, "Miss you."

Olivia interpreted the reduction in the amount of text associated with her post as an indication that her grief was transitioning from very acute and intense to something that she could manage better in her everyday life. The fact that she could scroll back through her memorial postings to determine this speaks to the therapeutic possibility of integrating mobile-emotive analyses of social and mobile media use into more narrative approaches to grief work. Many US participants discussed how, with time, previously emotionally charged digital content did not carry as much significance for the user as it once did. It was easier for them to distance themselves psychologically from their digital linking object, and they visited certain digital archives less often. It was interesting to observe how, for some participants, their emotions and expressions via social and mobile media became less raw over time, yet for others, time intensified their mobile-emotive expressions.

Mobile-emotive rituals of transition highlight how the integration of loss into our daily lives is not something that we do alone. Sharing the process via social and mobile media, as well as having a device that we can use for reflection, provides an amazing vehicle through which we can begin to understand the narrative process of bereavement like never before. Grieving has become something that remains deeply personal, while also being an easily shared experience via social and mobile media. Even losses that were once stigmatized and hidden from view have become more widely acknowledged as a result of the ease through which digital content can be generated and shared. This openness to sharing can take on a sinister element when discussing the more forensic side of the use of digital content (as in the sharing of crime scene photos).

However, the ease with which someone can share sensitive material does not take away from the bravery required, especially on social media, to be "out" about losses that may be judged harshly by others. Mobile media allow for individual realities to be accepted on their own terms; individual accounts of experiences must now be accepted instead of insisting that "perceptions of reality must be shared in order to be considered valid" (Kalish and Reynolds 1973, 210). Despite this, many mobile media users still desire validation and become concerned about the perception of their use. This perception is often shaped by and through the comments that people make to social media postings (as well as the assumed impressions derived from a lack of response).

Some US participants felt that they were not as privileged as others to be able to express their grief openly, due to the circumstances surrounding their loss. For as much as social media can be a source of liberation and freedom of expression for some, it can be a painful trap of emotional suppression for others. The pressure to "do grief" via mobile media is about the expression of raw emotion and the space to offer condolences and support. It is also the space through which users must perform mobile-emotive rituals of transition. These rituals are the means through which the bereaved indicate to others that they are renewed, that they are reconciled with their loss, and that they have returned to "the living."

CONCLUSION: THE ROLE OF MOBILE MEDIA IN CREATING A "NEW NORMAL" AND THE EVOLUTION OF SELF

We have discussed how changes in mobile media use often mark a shift and transition in a loss experience. This acknowledgment of change happens first in the process of picking up the pieces. This part of the grieving process can take on the characteristics of "moving on" or, to some, it is the definition of resilience. However, if we are to embrace the idea of a continuation of bonds, a love that never ends, and a grief that never ends, then "moving on" is not the right term. Instead, this phase of grief must be discussed as a "new normal"—life as it is changed by loss and how we live within that change. Our use of mobile media can assist in this process. The typical routines of mobile media engagement have the potential to highlight shifts in the ordinary nature of everyday life.

As never before, we have the means to document, down to the instant, the moment when everything changed. Through our mobile devices we can revisit the last text messaging, the last social media post, the moment before it happened, and the ordinary moment after the event. We can retrace our digital steps and recapture gaps in our natural memory through the examination of our mobile-emotive selves. This data is hard to let go of. It keeps the loss near, and it helps one make sense of seemingly senseless moments.

At the center of all these processes is the meaning-making aspect of the grief and the ways in which transition in grieving can indicate an evolution of self (Neimeyer 2006). People are often changed and enhanced by significant losses, and they usually re-evaluate their life's priorities. They may put a greater emphasis on interpersonal relationships and feel as though the event has encouraged a level of strength, empathy, and maturity that they did not have prior to the loss. Unlike any other time before this, we have ready access to mobile-mediated tools through which we can narrate and reflect on this enhancement of self. In the next section of this book, "Ghosts in the Mobile," we focus more on the haunted nature of mobile-emotive content and the ways in which mobile media can extend and continue the bonds we have with our deceased loved ones and the digital specters they leave behind.

SECTION II

GHOSTS IN THE MOBILE

6

The Selfie Affect in Disasters

The ghost is not simply a dead or missing person, but a social figure and investigating it can lead to that dense site where history and subjectivity make social life. The ghost or the apparition is one form by which something lost, or barely visible, or seemingly not there to our supposedly well-trained eyes, makes itself known as apparent to us. In its own way, of course. The way of the ghost is haunting, and haunting is a very particular way of knowing what has happened or is happening. Being haunted draws us affectively, sometimes against our will and always a bit magically, into the structure of feeling of a reality we come to experience, not as cold knowledge, but as a transformative recognition. (Avery 2001, 8)

When Soo-hyun's brother failed to return home after the South Korean MV *Sewol* ferry disaster in which 250 people, predominantly high school children, were killed, Soo-hyun cradled her mobile phone constantly, as if the device was an extension of him. Adorned with her brother's picture as a screen saver, Soo-hyun's mobile phone contained a testament to his life: the individual text messages he had sent her, the group Kakao IMs, and the Facebook pages and photos. While she grappled with the unregulated waves of grief that flooded her whole body in the days, weeks, and months after the disaster, her mobile phone became a container—not only for her and her family's memorialization of her brother and part of a ritual around continuing their bonds in his afterlife, but also a vessel for the growing consolidation of collective grief within Korean culture in the aftermath of the disaster.

In the example of Soo-hyun, we see the mobile phone has become a shrine for channeling and consolidating individual and social waves of grief through its various "intimate publics" (as discussed in Chapter 1) across social and mobile media. It also plays a key symbolic role in the continuing bonds between the deceased and the mourners. As discussed in Chapter 5, the mobile phone is a remediation of older memorialization and epistolary devices such as the photo album and letters, while also being an extension across temporal and spatial boundaries (Brubaker, Hayes, and Dourish 2013). Mobile phones are a repository for hauntings of the hand and the heart, signaling the continuing bonds of attachment (Bowlby 1980) whereby grief does not end (Rosenblatt 2000).

In the aforementioned sinking of the *Sewol* on April 16, 2014, mobile phones functioned across multiple forms of haunting. They became repositories for damning camera phone footage, taken by the now deceased, of procedures gone wrong. With some of the movies taken by children as young as eight years old, the footage shows terrifying scenes of people panicking. These selfie movies were not about narcissism, but about the numbness and misrecognition that trauma can bring with it (Wendt 2014). They visualized collective trauma. Mobile media photography provides a vehicle for continuing these activities, while at the same time it uniquely allows for these activities to extend across temporal and spatial boundaries (Brubaker, Hayes, and Dourish 2013). Far from narcissist vehicles, these selfies were not only used to connect in moments of trauma and grief, but they also played a key role in mobilizing the Korean population into a collective action against the boat company and the government following the disaster (Mullen 2014; Choi 2014; Kim and Jeon 2014).

Here the camera phone footage not only provided a witness for court prosecutors and trauma-laden images for the families of the deceased, but it also functioned as highly effective memorials that quickly spread and consolidated global public outcry. The rawness of camera phone imagery, as mementos for lives unfairly taken, became fuel for the palpable grief felt worldwide (YouTube 2014). Parents across the world felt the unspeakable pain of watching a child's final image to the world. These images remind us of Roland Barthes's (1981) notion of the "punctum"; that is, the *emotional affect* of these images on spectators. For Barthes, it was important to distinguish the punctum from the photographer, and also from the object photographed, which he calls the "studium." The punctum is the affect that haunts us.

In this instance, the selfie is unmistakably embedded within the emotional texture of everyday life as an image of misrecognition in all its tragedy. Images and messages sent by the now deceased high school children to their parents and siblings about the unfolding tragedy sealed the mobile phone as the witness to the disaster. Here the mobile phone amplifies the haunting of loss and grief, entangling different modes of co-presence and representation.

As noted earlier, mobile media both remediate older rituals around memory and life as they reshape the practices of grief. Holding onto treasured objects and inducing after-death communication via letter writing are activities recognized now as a part of the grieving process (Klass, Silverman, and Nickman 1996). (We will discuss this after-death process more in the following chapter.) While photography has always had a complicated relationship with power, representation, and death (Barthes 1981; Sontag 1977; Deger 2008), the social life of mobile media is changing the relationship between memory, image ownership, and dissemination. What happens to Barthes's notion of punctum—originally used to talk about analog photography—in the context of digital and mobile photography that includes still photographs, moving images, and live video broadcasts? How does the witnessing across online and mobile media create different types of punctum effect and attendant mourning communities?

In this chapter, we explore the ways in which grief and loss are culturally specific, including an array of various social responses, rituals, and cultural prescriptions. We show how mobile media practices in and around loss need to be understood as both extending earlier memorial practices of the use of photography and creating new ways in which death and loss manifest within our daily lives. As we have noted, much research has been conducted on the role of the digital (Gibbs et al. 2013; Brubaker et al. 2012; Graham et al. 2013; Lingel 2013; Church 2013; Deger 2008, 2006) but not specifically on *mobile* media, which brings with it particular forms of affordances, affect, and Barthes's punctum. We explore these ideas through a case study of the *Sewol* disaster, in which mobile phones played a role as witness, repository, disseminator, memorial, and consolidator. As demonstrated in the *Sewol* disaster, mobile media practices like selfies and vlogs are being deployed by the soon-to-be-deceased, and thus become self-eulogies. In order to understand the complex role mobile data trails are creating in, and around, the deceased, we need to connect it to earlier photographic practices around representations of the dead. Then we turn to considering affect in and around mobile media memorialization, followed by the case study related to the *Sewol* disaster.

PHOTOGRAPHING THE DEAD: THE SELFIE-AS-EULOGY IN CONTEXT

Magnifying the intimate nature of mobile media, camera phone practices play a key role in the changing ways memory and image are experienced and shared. While camera phone images are shaped by mobile technologies, they also play into broader photographic tropes and genres (Palmer 2012; Zylinska 2015; Frohlich et al. 2002; Kindberg et al. 2005; Whittaker et al. 2010; Van House et al. 2005; van Dijck 2007). At the crossroads between the aesthetic and the social, camera phone practices can provide insight into contemporary digital media.

This phenomenon is magnified in the context of selfies as a barometer for changing relationships between media, memory and death (Senft and Baym 2015; Walker Rettberg 2014; Frosh 2014). Digital data provide new ways in which to construct one's life, death, and after-death (Stanyek and Piekut 2010; de Vries and Rutherford 2004; Veale 2003; Bollmer 2013; Bennett and Bennett 2000; Jones 2004). These insights are especially highlighted with mobile media as a witness, repository, disseminator, and magnifier of events. Within this process, new types of genres such as "selfies at funeral" signal emergent relations between intimacy, mobile media, etiquette, and affect (Nansen et al. 2015).

Photographing the dead, also known as "postmortem photography," became popular in the Victorian era. Postmortem photography, sometimes called *memento mori*, was also found to be popular in the late nineteenth century in Palestine, the Near East, and India (Mansour and Fawaz 2009). Tangible representations of loss became precious mementos. Most often taken when a young child had died, these photos marked the importance of the loss and served as a reminder of the loved one's existence. The daguerreotype represented in Figure 6.1 was sold on eBay as an example of a postmortem photograph. Highly collectable today, it sold for over US$2,600.

In addition to these photos, many people in the late 1800s would create jewelry—necklace cords, lockets, and other similar pieces—out of the hair of the deceased. Mourning jewelry became popular, and it was not uncommon to see someone wearing a bracelet entirely

Figure 6.1 An example of a postmortem daguerreotype from the 1850s (from eBay).

made out of the beloved's hair—intricately and carefully braided into a durable cord-like material (Sweeney 2014). These mementos were worn on the body as a constant reminder of the loss, and perhaps as a means through which the wearer could feel connected to the deceased—not unlike the linking objects discussed in Chapter 4. And, as in Chapter 4, here we emphasize that the wearability of mobile devices may serve in a similar capacity to wearing mourning jewelry, in that people are able to carry with them, and put on display, digital remnants and remains of their deceased loved ones.

In 1861, William Mumler credited himself with being the inventor of spirit photography when he discovered a "ghostly" image of a young girl in a portrait he had taken. A spiritualist circulated the photo as the first piece of concrete evidence of the presence of a spirit, and Mumler instantly became famous. He opened up a shop in New York City where he would pose people and take a photo of them utilizing a special technique whereby spirits would "show themselves" if they were present. He would charge people for the service whether or not there was a spirit present in the photo (Kutz 2013). His most famous client was Mary Todd Lincoln, the widow of President Abraham Lincoln.

No strangers to spiritualism, both President Lincoln and his wife participated in a sèance that Mrs. Lincoln held in the White House in an attempt to make contact with their son who had died at age twelve. After her husband's assassination, Mrs. Lincoln turned to Mumler for evidence that his spirit was still around her. In the photo Mumler took of Mrs. Lincoln (depicted in Figure 6.2), the deceased president "appeared." He is standing behind Mrs. Lincoln, with his hands on her shoulders. Mrs. Lincoln received much comfort from this photo, and Mumler was quick to circulate it as proof of the existence of Lincoln's ghost in response to the interest of the American public. Lincoln's "ghost" appeared in many venues after his assassination, and it occupied the imagination of people for years (Kutz 2013).

The circulation and distribution of Mumler's photo, and other examples or representations of Lincoln's spirit transcending physical death, brought much comfort to the grieving American public. Fascination with the paranormal would carry over in the West, well into the twenty-first century. The persistence of the paranormal is found in many other cultures. Convening with spirits is an occurrence reported the world over. With the distribution of photographic technology, the desire to integrate this technology into the capture of the spirit world is becoming universal.

Figure 6.2 William Mumler, Mary Todd Lincoln with the spirit of Abraham Lincoln. *(From the Lincoln Financial Foundation Collection, courtesy of the Allen County Public Library and Indiana State Museum.)*

Shinrei shashin (心霊写真) is the Japanese term for spirits that show themselves in photos. Rendering spirits and ghosts visible through the use of the camera fits into the understanding that what is invisible can become visible through some transitory medium (Chalfen 2008). People in Japan continue to see *shinrei shashin* as a source of thrill and excitement as well as fear. The ghosts that appear are often closely examined to determine whether they are known ancestors or just wandering spirits. The term *shinrei* means the spirit of someone who has recently died. If a *shinrei* shows up in a photo, it may mean that the person is not at rest and was not tended to properly by the living. With the saturation of photographic culture in Japan through the use of mobile camera phones, the chances of capturing *shinrei shashin* have increased, and many people, young people especially, have become fascinated with the prospect of rendering this invisible world visible through their mobile devices (Chalfen 2008).

This phenomenon is best demonstrated by the success of the Ninetendo 3DS game called *Shinrei Camera* in 2012. The game has now been distributed worldwide, but its first market was in Japan, where it was developed by the Japanese gaming company Koei Tecmo. Beyond the game's main storyline and general gameplay, the game contains a feature called "haunted visions," by which the 3DS becomes a "spirit camera." Utilizing the camera inside the 3DS, the game allows players to take photographs of their surroundings in an effort to detect if any spirits are present. The game also has an augmented reality (AR) feature, by which, through the 3DS camera, ghosts are projected onto the player's current surroundings and the player must battle them (Riley 2012). The AR feature allows players to extend their experience of the game into what is occurring around them. The ways in which the projected digital content serves as an overlay not seen by others and only shared with players highlights the dual reality within which mobile media users are allowed to function. Augmented reality is where parameters of the technology then inspire the creativity of the user. Augmented reality cultivates a dissociative imaginative world where spirits are allowed to exist and the bereaved may convene with a portal to the "other side."

Making contact with the souls of the departed is not a new concept or practice, especially among cultures with some of the most tangible ties to ancient ancestors. Being able to make contact with a lost loved one in the spirit realm often brings solace to the bereaved. Sometimes people seek to make contact in order to have an unanswered question resolved or to gain reassurance that their loved one has "crossed over" peacefully to the spirit world, that they are intact (sometimes even better than when they were alive), and that they are always present— (most times) invisible and silent, but present (Kutz 2013).

In the past, people would employ nonverifiable techniques of "contact" and spirits would make their presence known through some form of "communication"—the flickering of lights, strange noises, tapping, the movement of a glass, automatic movement of a pen on paper, the Ouija Board, and so on. These examples demonstrate how the ordinary can become infused with the extraordinary—in essence, another take on augmented reality. In similar ways, the mobile device as typical, ubiquitous, and everyday can take on fantastical dimensions as a vehicle through which communication with the spirit world, through mobile-emotive memorialization practices, can be imagined and felt. In the next section, we discuss the move from the hauntings of the hand in terms of photography to understanding these memorialization processes in terms of affect.

HAUNTINGS OF THE HAND: MOBILE-EMOTIVE MEMORIALIZATION

Rather than being a place of internalization, of quiet contemplation, the Web memorial answers the question of what the bereaved are thinking and feeling, at times communicating "wrenching expressions of grief and loss." . . . The visual, material, and semiotic evidence presented here also points to online memorials remaining secular and possibly as marking a re-emergence of the "cult of the dead" (Ariès 1981, 208), when the dead are celebrated. Importantly, a whole series of grieving and memorialization practices, some of which would otherwise remain ephemeral and private, are made visible, durable, and public through online memorials. (Graham et al. 2015, 51)

As Graham et al. observe, binaries between "old" offline gravesites and "new" online memorials miss the complexities of understanding how all-pervasive grief and bereavement are. Rather, the online and offline are entangling processes of remediation—that is, a dynamic interplay between online and offline, old and new rituals—that are part of a transformation in how we understand, experience, and practice grief and loss (Graham et al. 2015, 52). Moving beyond binary distinctions, and instead understanding different forms of representation as part of a tapestry, is also important when thinking about intimacy and emotion.

As Sara Ahmed (2004) notes in the case of the "cultural politics of emotion," we need to move beyond binary Western models of emotion as inside/outside and instead understand its affective capacity that leaves residue on the texture of the body. Ahmed explores the work that the lived emotions do in and around the capitalist nation-state and how emotion works on the surfaces of bodies. For Ahmed, emotions have affective power (2004, 60). In her discussion of fear and grief, Ahmed argues that emotions stick to bodies that in turn carry these particular histories and memories. This relationship between emotion, grief, and affect is most apparent in the *Sewol* disaster, in which mobile images operated as self-designated eulogies for the high school children who were tragically killed. These selfie images spoke to a new type of punctum, a mobile punctum, whereby immediacy, ubiquity, and intimacy are entangled within the sticky aesthetics of the affect.

Writing two years after the *Sewol* disaster, one can feel the haunting of a country still in mourning for all those young, unlived lives. The mobile media specters are haunted with punctum residue. As the grief goes through a variety of shades and depths, we see a country struggling with the reality of the disaster. During and after the disaster, mobile phones functioned in a pivotal way to generate not only complex ways in which we might understand the entanglements between co-presence and deadness, but also the ways in which grief and loss (and those lost) can be channeled and memorialized in new and remediated ways. Mobile media become haunted vessels for and of grief. They become interlocutors between liveness and deadness across multiple forms of presence, co-presence, and telepresence.

As mentioned in Chapter 2, much of mobile media literature, through the work of the STS sociologist Licoppe and anthropologist Ito, has discussed the importance of understanding mobile media intimacy in terms of co-presence; that is, as sense of electronic proximity when physically apart. However, this co-presence can be further extended in the case of deadness or afterlife. As Jason Stanyek and Benjamin Piekut note, the performances of deadness within digitality are

> spurred into being through the portended traces of too many histories to name and too many futures to subsume in a stable, locatable present . . . the topologies of deadness—those never-ending emplacements with concatenations of displacements— are patterned and repatterned through specific arrangements of co-labor, or the interpenetrating, distributed effectivities of all entities that have effects. (2010, 19–20)

As Brubaker, Hayes, and Dourish note in "Beyond the Grave: Facebook as a Site for the Expansion of Death and Mourning," "social networking sites enable expansion—temporally, spatially, and socially—of public mourning. Rather than looking at online practices as disruptions of traditional practices of grief and memorialization, we examine them as new sites in which public mourning takes place" (2013, 152). In "Millions Now Living Will Never Die: Cultural Anxieties about the Afterlife of Information," Grant Bollmer writes that

> death online—defined as the persistence of informatics remainders after the death of the human user—reveals how networked data are constructed as both an authentic duplicate of identity and as a threat to personal identity that must be managed. Because humans are understood as finite and mortal, while data are immortal and everlasting, the "life" formed out of online data is understood as beyond any possible control of the user. (2013, 142)

This binary between human and data (nonhuman), and between life and death, is a pervasive one. As Bollmer observes, technologies have always "externalized sensory data, transforming human consciousness and conceptions of the self" (2013, 144). He notes, drawing from the work of Derrida and Stiegler (2002) and Sconce (2000), that each "new technology, which stores and externalizes sensory data in a new way, is also seen as that which makes present specific reminders of those who have passed on" (Bollmer 2013, 144). For phenomenologists, data cannot be separated from the human and the embodied experience. While online media remediate and amplify the ability of technology to bring the deceased back to life, they also bring new affordances, hauntings and modes of co-presence:

> That technology seems to bring the deceased back to life is not something unique to network technology. Recordings have always animated traces of the deceased. What is new about network technology is the belief that the amount of data recorded and externalized gives a nearly full representation of the authentic identity of the human being. It is not simply the presence of the deceased that causes anxiety, but the supposed fullness of

that presence, formed by near-totalized recording, networked and beyond the control of the user. (2013, 145)

As Bollmer identifies, our lives are increasingly leaving data-heavy digital trails. So how do we think about this data when it comes to afterlife? What stories do data reveal about our lives? And what stories do they ignore? As mobile devices entangle us in a type of thick digital co-presence in and of our lives, what digital traces will live on after we pass away? Once upon a time, when someone passed away, their loved ones would come and clean up their material possessions. But, as a continuation of the previous chapter, how does one clean up the digital specters that feel so omnipresent and ubiquitous, especially when the use or preservation of those digital specters are not completely under our control? In the next section, we explore the case study of the Korean ferry disaster in which mobile media played a key role in the collective trauma and affect, impacting both the intimate and public in various ways.

INTIMATE AND MEMORIALIZED PUBLICS: MOBILE MEDIA AFFECT IN THE *SEWOL* DISASTER

As soon as the ferry *Sewol* capsized on April 16, 2014, multiple mobile phones were on hand capturing the sheer terror of the events unfolding. While a few of these stories were documented and disseminated in global press via translation from Hangul to English (as depicted in Figure 6.3), dozens of stories of mobile media memorialization processes remained untranslated and were shared only on local Korean sites and between users most impacted by the tragedy. After the boat sunk and over 250 schoolchildren died from drowning or hypothermia, it was the mobile media footage that friends and family cradled in disbelief. YouTube began to

Figure 6.3 In Western media, pictures of family members overwhelmed with grief symbolized 2014.04.16 (YouTube screenshot).

fill with hundreds of UCC videos, consolidating public anger and outcry. As depicted in Figure 6.4, most traumatic were the mobile media fragments of children who had left messages to their parents that they loved them just as the reality of the situation started to dawn on them. Through these highly distressing messages, a process of grief and loss had begun for both the now deceased and the families left behind.

While much of the literature on bereavement and online memorials focuses upon the loss and experiences of the mourner, the Korean ferry disaster provided some examples of the role of the soon-to-be-deceased in mobile media memorialization. The quotidian and intimate dimension of mobile media undoubtedly impact processes of grief differently than other media. In the disaster, many families were receiving messages and videos from their children unaware that these fragments would be the last moments captured of their children's

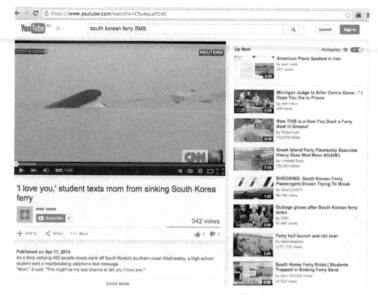

Figure 6.4 "This might be my last chance to tell you I love you" (A son's last message to his mother) (YouTube screenshot).

lives. Here mobile-mediated co-presence took on new dimensions in its ability to traverse physical distance and engender psychological closeness alongside its ability to traverse the mortal and immortal.

The story of the tragedy also unfolded in the description of procedures gone wrong. Documentation of this, through the use of mobile media, allowed others to redeploy the material to serve not only as a memorial, but also as a way in which to learn from the tragedy. As can be seen in the one of the most viewed YouTube clips, "What happened inside *Sewol* ferry 2014.04.16" (see Figure 6.5), mobile media from the deceased was used not only to continue bonds with *intimates*, but also to serve *public* justice in the wake of their deaths. The replaying and editing of the mobile footage served to further formalize and legitimate the collective role of grief and the need to acknowledge grief's unending nature. In the re-editing of the mobile footage,

Figure 6.5 What happened inside Sewol ferry 2014.04.16 (YouTube screenshot).

specters were allowed to live on and memorialization was allowed to cohabitate various online and offline spaces.

While the remixing of the mobile footage of the deceased afforded different ways for people to participate in the memorialization process globally, it also signaled a particular type of relational bond specific to Korean culture. Here it is important to understand how grief is shaped by culturally specific notions and rituals. As mentioned in Chapter 1, within Western contexts, grief has not only been individualized and privatized, but it has also been compartmentalized. In his social constructivist approach, Rosenblatt (2000) argues that we must understand that grief varies in social responses and cultural prescriptions. In Korea, grief must be understood in terms of *jeong*. Here the concept of *jeong* is significant as one of the most "endearing and evocative" words for which there is no English equivalent (Kim 1996). This is not to essentialize experience, but rather to understand the specific cultural milieu from which the grief was formed. As Luke Kim notes,

> *Jeong* encompasses the meaning of a wide range of English terms: feeling, empathy, affection, closeness, tenderness, pathos, compassion, sentiment, trust, bonding and love. . . . Koreans considers *jeong* an essential element in human life, promoting the depth and richness of personal relations. . . . In times of social upheaval, calamity, and unrest, *jeong* is the only binding and stabilizing force in human relationships. Without *jeong*, life would be emotionally barren and a person would feel isolated and disconnect from others. (1996, 14)

While a similar notion of *jeong* can be found in Chinese and Japanese culture (i.e., *jyo*), it has a far less significant and poignant meaning (Kim 1996). The feeling of *jeong* is palpable in and through the tragic events and memorialization of the disaster. A free telephone number (#1111) was established for people to send a text message in living memory of the victims. Over a four-day period, from April 25 to April 28, 2014, about 87,000 messages were sent to this number (*Yonhap News* 2014).

The mobile footage of the disaster still leaves a raw affect in that it captures the pain, confusion, and terror of the victims as they faced their deaths. The role of mobile media to capture this liminal stage is a testament to its intimate and ubiquitous role. Unquestionably, this area of mobile media memorialization before death will continue to grow and become a key area for analysis in the future. Given the newness of this phenomenon, in this section we will detail some of the events and the mobile media fragments produced as we consider the changing role of mobile media in and through moments of life, death, and afterlife. We will demonstrate the ways in which mobile-emotive media remediates old forms of spirit photography, whereby the deceased can now appear suddenly, sometimes unexpectedly, and often hauntingly on one's screen—in essence, witnessing practices become haunted.

One of the most traumatic issues surrounding the tragedy was that this event shouldn't have happened. The boat company took on too many passengers, and not enough lifeboats were stored onboard. The water was so cold that passengers died within minutes of being submerged. The company didn't call rescue boats immediately, and passengers alerting their friends and families to the accident did nothing to change this fact. In the confusion that prevailed, mobile phones captured an ambient fear and palpable terror through video footage, camera phone images, text messages, and IMs. One of the most tragic pieces of video footage is of a conversation recorded by the student Park Ye-seul, who filmed the disaster at 9:40 a.m. (the disaster was first reported at 8:40 a.m.). Her father recovered the footage from her mobile phone after her death.

The video conversation, which can now be found on YouTube, consists of a conversation between Ye-seul and other ferry passengers, as well as her co-present parents. She talks about how scared she and other passengers are, while begging, "Please rescue us." She talks about the increasing tilt of the boat. Then there is an official announcement relayed in the video, "Please double-check your life jacket, whether it is tightened well or not. Please check and tighten it again." Ye-seul says to her videoing phone (as if her parents are inside it), "Oh we're going to dive into the water," followed by "Mum, I am so sorry. Sorry Dad! It's bullshit!! We will be okay! See you alive" (YouTube, Ye-seul video, 2014).

When Ye-seul's father recovered his daughter's smartphone after the disaster, he dried it out and replaced the SIM card. On the phone were videos she had filmed during the disaster. For her father, the phone was not just a vessel for channeling a re-enactment of her last moments alive—it also afforded him the ability to feel co-presently with her during her last moments. In these postmortem moments, the power of the phone cannot be underestimated.

We also see that Ye-seul's selfies are far from a vehicle for narcissism. Here we see how selfies can be viewed as a barometer for changing relationships between media, memory, and death (Senft and Baym 2015; Walker Rettberg 2014; Frosh 2014). They are, as noted earlier, about a numbness and misrecognition of the event (Wendt 2014). They become part of the process of memorialization for her family and friends, specters of *jeong* while the deceased is still alive. Here, again, we see how powerful the mobile phone is, that it is one of the most intimate devices to capture the fleeting moments of the deceased before they pass away—a remediation of postmortem photography. For loved ones, not unlike those of the nineteenth century, mobile media become a crucial embodied part of the passage from life to death and afterlife.

For Si-yeon Kim's father, it was the mobile phone accompanying his daughter's body that held the key to her last moments. Here the mobile phone becomes an incubator for loved ones to connect with the last moments of the deceased's life over and over again. Like many of her fellow students who died, Si-yeon used her phone to not only document the tragedy as it unfolded, but also as a vehicle for memorializing her last moments for her loved ones. In the video, Si-yeon shows how urgent and dangerous the situation was by filming the chaos. At the end of the video, she prays for other people on the ferry. Even though she wasn't rescued, she worried about other passengers (YouTube, Si-yeon Kim video, 2014).

The role of the mobile phone in continuing bonds between the living and the dead was evidenced in a scenario between a deceased son and his father on Kakao IM. Here the mobile phone became a medium and a portal between Earth and the afterlife. In traditional Korean funereal practice, it is not uncommon for mourning relatives and friends to send messages to the deceased to continue the bonds and *jeong*. This tradition is demonstrated and remediated by one father's use of his deceased son's phone number as a portal. The father sent messages of grief to his son's number (Kakao.com 2014), such as:

> 1:40 p.m.
> How are you my little baby?
> I must have sinned a lot so that's why it happened to you. I am so sorry my little baby. Could you please forgive me? yeah?
> . . . .
> When I get old and die to go to meet you, please don't forget about your dad, yeah?
> . . .
> I love you.
> I love you so so much.
> You know how much I love you, my little baby?

However, the idea that his son's Kakao number could have been given to someone else had not been considered when one day he received a reply:

> I'm doing well. Please take care and be happy Daddy. And I am really fine so please live a long and healthy life. I love you!

After the father's initial shock that someone had responded to his son's old number, the father and the stranger continued to converse. The exchange between the two is one of great intimacy, highlighting that mobile media create multiple forms of intimate publics in which intimate strangers may bond.

Mobile media footage functioned as specters of a tragedy and for the continuing *jeong*. The deceased passenger Dong Hyuk Kim left a video letter to his family on his phone before the ferry sunk. His mother sent him a video letter after he passed away. The following transcript is a condensed version of Dong Hyuk Kim's video and his mother's later voice-over:

0:03: Mom. . .
0:04: Dad. . .
0:07: Oh my younger sister. . .
0:09: Mom and Dad! I love you!
0:13: To my son, Dong Hyuk Kim [mom's voice-over].
My lovely son, Dong Hyuk, a son like an angel. You worried about your younger sister and you said I love you Mom and Dad as the last video letter. Thank you so much.
Thank you my son to be my son and to live as your mom forever.
Dong Hyuk, please help us to find missing people who were still in the water and come back to their mom and dad.
To my son Dong Hyuk, I'm so sorry that I couldn't be with you while you were having the toughest time. And I promise I will be with your good dad, younger sister that you worried.
1:20: My son, My little baby, Kim Dong Hyuk!
I love you so much, Dong Hyuk. (YouTube, Dong Hyuk, 2014)

The function of social and mobile media to continue bonds and extend pathways for after-death communication and grieving was demonstrated by the use of various platforms from Korean-specific Kakao to global platforms like Facebook. Someone went to the group memorial altar and read a letter written by one of the victims' mother to her beloved daughter. This person wanted to share this letter with others, and posted it on their Facebook feed. Many of the stories that prevailed highlighted a contestation between traditional media stories and social media.

For example, there is the tragic story of Hyun-jin, a student whose father—believing Hyun-jin had been rescued, based on Kakao IM

Figure 6.6 Kakao IM and a photo sent from Hyun-jin to his father. (*Images from http://www.sisainlive.com/news/quickViewArticleView.html?idxno=20058.*)

received from his son (see Figure 6.6)—reported that information on Kakao, only to find out later he had not survived. After much mobile media correspondence on the evening of April 15, and the following morning, Hyun-jin's father's last conversation with his son took place at 9:15 a.m., when Hyun-jin sent a picture of himself in a life jacket. At 11:30 a.m. that day, Hyun-jin's father, believing the news reports that everyone had been rescued from the sunken ferry, posted on his Kakao Story, "My son was on the way to Jeju-island for his field trip and there was an incident!! News said everyone was rescued safely but I'm still worrying ." That morning TV news reported that there was an incident on the *Sewol* ferry, but that everyone was rescued safely.

In the hours and days following those first reports, the reality of the disaster was revealed. Hyun-jin's father went to the port to wait many days for his son's body to be retrieved. During this time, he posted a diary on his Kakao Story. As the nation tried to deal with the grief and guilt of the disaster, stories transpired about now-deceased ferry passengers sending their loved ones messages of *jeong*. Along with individual IM, some passengers used the Kakao Talk group chat for teachers and students to communicate during the event. One group chat consisted of thirty-nine members (including one teacher and thirty-eight students). The students were from a second form class at Danwon High School in Ansan, South Korea. While some of these participants were rescued, many did not survive.

CONCLUSION: MOBILE-EMOTIVE MEMORIALS AND PUNCTUM

> We photograph things in order to drive them out of our minds. My stories are a way of shutting my eyes. (Franz Kafka, cited in Barthes 1981)

As mentioned previously, Roland Barthes wrote what is arguably one of the most poetic explorations of photography, *Camera Lucida* (1981). He wrote this book while he was mourning his mother. In the book, he engages with the complicated relationship between representation and memory. Unquestionably, *Camera Lucida* was a book as much about death as it was about photography. It is a study of subjectivity and vulnerability. While Barthes wrote it as a eulogy for his mother, it ended up also being a eulogy for him, with his death from complications from an automobile accident happening only two months after it was published. In writing about the role of photography and death, Barthes conjures Kafka.

However, in a digital and mobile world, do the narratives we make—whether visual, textual, or verbal—allow us to shut our eyes? Here Barthes is highlighting the entanglement between photography and memory. And yet, in an accelerated time of rapid camera-phone picture taking and sharing, how does this reshape the relationship between memory and photography? Can all the selfies we take be a way of driving the experiences out of our mind and toward an intimate public to attempt to understand, as Wendt (2014) argues, the numbness of the moment?

The role of media in constructing and narrating someone's life and death has a long, complicated history. While focusing on the rise of the nation-state and the demise of the vernacular through the birth of the printing press, Benedict Anderson's *Imagined Communities* (1982) points to one account of how media has mediated our lives and deaths. However, with mobile and digital media, we see how the rise of the vernacular creates intimate publics. With multiple devices and platforms, across numerous intimate and unfamiliar publics, our data weaves stories that are not necessarily the narrative we see as our life. But, in the end, does this new media really change how a life is remembered and then memorialized after death?

As suggested in this chapter, mobile media extends both earlier media representation practices like photography, and the printing press and culturally specific notions like *jeong*, while also extending, expanding, and transforming rituals around life and death in ways we are still trying to understand fully. Much like the analog camera once did, mobile media are becoming interwoven with the rituals in and around living and dying. When discussing the *Sewol* disaster and the effect of the mobile-emotive eulogy-selfies, we are reminded of how the punctum now takes on a type of affective networked witnessing unimagined in the analog world.

Much like the high school children in this chapter's case study, the ability of mobile media images to create a type of punctum effect is clear. The slightly blurred images and the faceless audio streams produced by many mobile media during the disaster have created a new tapestry between the studium and the punctum. The selfie images taken by the students not only became highly politicized in an amplified sense of studium (that is, the object of the photograph), but they also resonated such posthumous punctum that it is hard not to be physically shaken by their affect. Moreover, we see how punctum combines with the Korean-specific notion of *jeong* to create a particularly unique Korean experience of the tragedy.

In the aftermath of the *Sewol* disaster, various forms of public online memorials—denoted by a yellow ribbon—were established on social media sites such as Kakao Talk, Kakao Story, and Facebook, and on interactive websites that sought to remix content, stories and memories. The yellow ribbon campaign aimed to provide a *jeong* solidarity. The icon was designed by the local Korean college student association at the Ansan high school that lost so many of its students. In the process of memorialization, mobile media featured predominantly as the content, frame, and context. As noted earlier, while some stories appeared in global Western media, many of the mobile media memorializations stayed untranslated in Hangul. We have focused upon these untranslated stories to give a sense of the localized intimacy mobile media can provide.

The *Sewol* disaster put in action a phenomenon that will become more pervasive in everyday life: the use of mobile media as visual eulogy by dying individuals and the possibility of the live broadcasting of death. As mentioned above, much of the literature referenced focuses upon the digital traces and specters left by those departed, rather than exploring how those facing death deploy mobile media to create their own mobile-emotive obituary. As mobile media become increasingly deployed, documenting and sharing death, as much as life, will become more apparent. When we leave behind digital trails, we must ask which are residual and which become ephemeral ghosts. Will the significance and affect produced by mobile media surrounding the way we die overshadow the significance of how we lived?

Mobile media is undoubtedly extending earlier rituals around death and afterlife as it is providing new avenues for creating digital intimate publics. The multiple and contesting digital specters allow for friends and family to curate and customize ways for memorialization. Social media allows people to share an experience across different temporalities and spatialities (and imagined spiritual dimensions).

However, this sharing is uneven, and those that broadcast their experiences the loudest are not necessarily those that feel the most pain. This disparity can amplify the unevenness of the intimate public, whereby commenting may not equate with closeness. The magnifying of these uneven stories and their relationship to intimacy is a debate that will only continue to grow.

Along with Kakao Talk and Facebook, other online informal memorial sites for victims of the *Sewol* disaster blossomed from Korean search engine companies like Daum and Naver (such as ordering/offering online flower symbols, in keeping with offline Korean traditions). Just as flowers are placed on the offline memorial sites, online flower *emoji* gifts could be posted to online memorials on Kakao and Facebook. There was even an interactive memorial site that attempted to narrate particulars of the tragedy through a collage of media such as videos, photos, and interviews. There is an online memorial site with illustrated portraits and stories of each victim; a smartphone case for remembrance; and 20140416 bracelets. Unquestionably, mobile media played a pivotal role in the processes of memorialization. From the images and messages sent to families and friends as intimate gestures to the public outrage and protest in the aftermath, mobile media highlights the ways in which memorialization can provide intimate publics.

As mentioned previously, writing this during the two-year anniversary of the event, it is clear that the grief remains palpable in Korea. However, after the suicide of the boat company owner, Koreans have transformed their grief into anger, and the topic has become deeply political. It will be interesting to see how the stories of mobile media memorialization operate as sites for family and loved ones to continue their connection and *jeong* between their loved ones in the afterlife. One thing remains clear: mobile media is playing an increasingly pivotal role in the continuing bonds between loved ones and the deceased, as well as providing various forms of intimate publics across global and local media. The next chapter extends some of the points raised in this chapter and highlights the ways in which mobile media becomes a medium through which the deceased can be channeled and connections continued.

7

Open Channeling and Continuity

Magic too is a myth but myths shape our machines into meanings. (Davis 1998, 189)

It is like your mobile phones, [cell phones]. Well you have cell phones to your loved ones in the spirit land. You do not need a number, all you have to do is reach out to them with love and affection and they answer your call. You may not always be aware of them but I assure you they answer your call, they are with you. That is why you must look upon them with love and affection my friends. (Spirit Guide Hai 2006)

The website *Speaking Spirits* featured this channeled message of the Spirit Guide Hai during a spirit communication at the Celebration Centre and Metaphysical Society in Penticton, Canada, in October 2006. Hai described channeling by using mobile communication as a metaphor to represent the nature of communicating with the dead. As this quote demonstrates, the wireless nature of mobile communication makes it amenable to a comparison with communication in the spirit realm. The intimate nature through which we can literally hear the voice of another in our heads—seamlessly, wirelessly, anywhere, at anytime—allows for some to make an easy connection to how "spirit" is channeled through mobile media. Cheri Barstow (2010) has described this idea:

Let's think of channeling as a cell/mobile phone into another world. The channeler can't see the person on the other end of the line but they can hear them. They are just as real to them as if they were a friend calling from across town. They can hear them just as clearly and the connection is made whenever they need to communicate.

The mobile communication metaphor allows for the existence of an invisible realm around our practical reality. It gives credence to the notion that there may be multiple realms of communication co-occurring at the same time. The integration of wireless technology into our everyday lives further elucidates the struggle, as some believe, of living at the crux of the material and immaterial worlds. As fantastical as this may seem, this is the foundation of many of the belief systems of the world's religions—that there exists some benevolent, omnipotent spiritual force just beyond our awareness, invisible to us but somehow still connected. In this chapter we will explore some of the influences on traditional and modern-day mortuary practices as a means toward understanding how mobile media participate, at times, in the cultivation of a haunted culture. Through the use of examples from the interviews conducted in the United States, we will further demonstrate how mobile media can become the vehicle through which after-death communication can take place and a mobile-emotive continuation of bonds can occur.

CULTURAL INFLUENCES AND BELIEFS IN IMMORTALITY AND TRADITIONAL MORTUARY PRACTICE

As mentioned previously in this book, we are encountering death as a cultural, spiritual, historical, and social phenomenon, as well as a deeply psychological one. In discussing issues related to mobile media use and death, grieving, and the dead, it is important to recognize the role that Western perspectives and Anglocentric belief systems have had in influencing the cultural blending that has occurred related to more traditional and localized mortuary practices worldwide. And while we do not want to reify the East-West binary, Western ideological dominance can be found in mainstream psychological approaches to dealing with grief and loss. Dying itself, of course, is a universal phenomenon—one that has been grappled with from the dawn of human existence. And bearing witness to the loss of a loved one is the natural counterpart to the universality of death.

Throughout the world, the many traditions surrounding death are often reflective of dominant religious identities. Cultivation of religious ideology often occurs in juxtaposition to cultural norms and folk traditions, especially as it relates to the dead and the process of mourning. As Antonius Robben stated, "A central theme of interdisciplinary inquiry has been the tension between the inevitability of death and the belief in spiritual immortality" (2004, 2). A belief in the existence of life after death has been found to fall into two main categories: literal immortality and symbolic immortality. Literal immortality focuses on the belief in an afterlife based on the immortality of an individual's soul. This kind of immortality is what is commonly understood through cultural and spiritual rituals and practices: that upon death there is a separation between body and soul, and that even after the physical death of the body, the soul persists. In symbolic immortality, existence beyond death is achieved through the maintenance and extension of one's life's work into the culture that one leaves behind. In this, a person can live forever through their deeds and the contributions they made in life and through the ways in which they are remembered by the living (Ai et al. 2014).

While the teachings may vary in terms of how extensive their knowledge of the afterlife is, none of the teachings of the world's major religions promote the idea that death is an end (Code and Poston 2015). In other words, we may not know exactly what happens after we die, but the idea that continued existence may be possible comes to shape how the majority of people grieve. In fact, mobile devices are now a part of some traditional mortuary practices, as US participant Wei (19, Chinese) revealed about traditions in China. He explained how people in China understand the importance of having a mobile phone in the afterlife:

> People make an iPhone out of paper and they burn them [at the funeral] and [they] think that stuff goes to them [in the after-life]. . . . They just think that the dead person might need those things, so they buy those paper stuff to burn it and like send it to them. It's kind of weird. They think that on the other side they can use [the paper iPhone] to communicate.

People of all cultures are attempting to integrate the presence of mobile technology into traditional practices. This is just another example of how people continue to struggle with reconciling the needs of the dead with those of the living. It is a near universal spir-itual belief that mistreatment of the dead could mean a soul remains unsettled for eternity. Across the globe, the handling of the dead is often left to funeral professionals, emphasizing that what happens to the deceased in the time immediately following the death is very important to most mourners. In Japan, protecting the dead body from harm is of utmost importance until the funeral ceremony is over. The finality of death does not come until the death rituals are complete. This means the body is handled with great care, and that it is well prepared for its final journey to the other world (Suzuki 2004).

It is also quite common across many cultures that not showing the proper respect or display of grief by the living for the deceased could lead to public shaming and condemnation from one's com-munity. As a result, even today, on spiritual, cultural, and social (and sometimes public health) levels, the dead pose dangers to the living

(Malinowski 2005). This feeling further highlights what endures today and is made evident through mobile media practices: the tension and trepidation between the living and the dead, and the ways in which death can be at once holy yet haunting—sacred yet septic.

The living's attachment to the dead and the ways in which the dead assist and protect the living are ancient beliefs common to many cultures, especially those in the East. The continuation and adaptation of ancient cultural rituals in modern life have been studied as a means of negotiating the divide between attempts at preserving culture and the anxieties associated with modernity (Pearce 2011). Contemporary engagements with the spirit world, what Pearce (2011) calls "disincarnate entities," become a way that quasi-indigenous practices can become reimagined in the present and a vehicle through which we collectively cultivate a "haunted culture."

CULTIVATION OF A HAUNTED CULTURE

Despite the fact that most of academia is dominated by empiricism and the role of the scientific method in defining what reality is, there still exists a belief in the paranormal that appears to be quite universal (Partridge 2013). Ghosts and disincarnate spirits are a part of the lives of both modern and traditional peoples (Pearce 2011). The bereaved especially are allowed to suspend their disbelief and indulge in magical thinking. This permission by rational society to allow for a belief in paranormal experience is granted more to those whose experiences are interpreted as being metaphorical or as mere extensions of their inner worlds. There is more resistance by the rational public to accept paranormal experiences when those experiences are being presented as actual phenomena (Jenzen and Munt 2013).

Acceptance of these experiences as being a part of how individuals cope with traumatic events further emphasizes the value that modern society places on the inner worlds of the individual. This Western orientation of valuing of psychological experiences of the individual and the maintenance of "the self" is a marked development of the twentieth century that has come to shape our current age. Beyond the distraction of securing life's most basic needs, individuals who are privileged enough to occupy the space of post-material society now place their focus on the development of the self and the accumulation and valuation of experience (Partridge 2013).

This movement toward self-exploration and self-discovery took hold in the United States in the 1960s. The development of existential and humanistic branches of psychology had, deep within it, the influence of theosophical and Eastern notions of the transcendence of self and the seeking of peak experiences whereby one may connect and extend the self beyond the limits of the physical and material realm (Rogers 1980). These aspects of "selfhood" are metaphysical and often require the imagination of the individual to enact. Transcending the self challenges the limits of human existence and opens the door for the creation of a sense of self that is limitless and, ultimately, ceaseless. If we strive to occupy this notion of self, a boundless, endless self, we must suspend typical ties to practical reality and move beyond that which is verifiable through empirical methods—one definition of paranormal. The cultivation of and connection to paranormal experiences shape and surround everything in the material world. In essence, there is what Christopher Partridge calls an occulture co-existing within ontological reality:

> Occulture, as a sociological term, refers to the environment within which, and the social processes by which particular meanings relating, typically, to spiritual, esoteric, paranormal and conspiratorial ideas emerge, are disseminated, and become influential in societies and in the lives of individuals. Central to these processes is popular culture, in that it disseminates and remixes

occultural ideas, thereby incubating new spores of occultural
thought. (Partridge 2013, 116)

This occulture is a part of culture that is somewhat secretive and not
readily admitted to. Many individuals, especially in the acute phases
of grief, keep secret the ways in which they may engage in or discover
connections to the paranormal or ideas that feel out of the ordinary. Again, these experiences could be explained away as responses
to trauma and a result of the heartbreak of loss. However, for the
individual experiencing it, it becomes real-yet-invisible, present-
yet-illusive, and validating-yet-invalid on all rational levels.
Paranormal experiences are situated in the normal and the ordinary.
"Contact" usually occurs in particular places. Places and objects then
become the matter of hauntings. And, if as the result of the integration of mobile media into the everyday, spaces become transitory,
augmented, virtual, and immaterial, why wouldn't it be logical to
assume that the devices themselves could become "haunted," too?
Since most people are curious about the paranormal and experiences
outside the realm of ontological reality, we are able to explore the
ways in which mobile technology is being used metaphorically, and
at times literally, to assist in connecting with this "spiritual" or invisible realm of the dead.

IN PURSUIT OF A MOBILE-EMOTIVE PSYCHOMANTEUM

In the times before photography and the moving image, reflective
surfaces such as shiny stones, the surface of water, and, later, glass
and mirrors were used as a source for generating visions and seeing
into the unseen, spiritual realms (Moody 1992). Spaces—private,
separate, and apart from more public domains—were constructed

to assist in facilitating these visions. Known as *psychomanteums*—or theaters of the mind—the ancient Greeks created these spaces to be like sensory deprivation chambers where sensory information was limited: the lights low, the space covered in black, no natural light used, with only the light of a candle or lamp and a mirror present. These conditions were seen as optimal for being able to see a vision, to receive messages, and to connect visually with a departed loved one (Moody 1992). The space generated a heightened state of awareness as well as a deep sense of intimacy and privacy. This connection was experienced as deeply emotional, and most people who reported this kind of experience appeared changed by it.

The nature of mobile communication may make it easily adaptable to serve as a modern-day, mobile-emotive psychomanteum. The conditions under which people report feeling the presence of lost loved ones via their mobile device typically occur in a similar fashion—in times when they are alone, often absent of other sensory distractions. The intimate space generated between the user and the device is not unlike the intimate space generated between the bereaved and the mirror in the psychomanteum.

While not necessarily literal, the metaphor of the mobile-emotive psychomanteum is presented here as a means through which the reader can generate a sense that people who utilize the technology in this way are seeking this kind of connection. They desire to stay in contact and in communication with lost loved ones beyond death. Often, this sense of connection occurs in the quiet time spent alone with one's device. The ever-presence of the device can lend itself to traces of this connection enduring just outside the consciousness of the user. Namely, if the device is associated with an extraordinary experience, even in the ordinary it may retain its extraordinary qualities.

Again, we are not discussing these phenomena and beliefs as a means to prove their existence. Rather, we are acknowledging that these are commonly held understandings of the world, and there-fore have the potential to influence the use of mobile media. In fact, people are often reluctant to talk about these kind of phenomena out of fear of ridicule (Bennett and Bennett 2000; Dannenbaum and Kinnier 2009). This feeling was exemplified by the US partic-ipant Diamond (20, African American), who discussed her belief that when people pass away, their presence is still felt, a belief she quickly qualified to make sure she was in keeping with common beliefs:

> I feel like that is a mental thing of not being able to let go, like *you* still hold on to them, so *you* feel like they are still there, but I feel like with [the dead], they are still lingering like ghosts, that they didn't reach to where they were supposed to go in life so they are still on Earth trying to figure out where to go. You know how some people will be like, "Oh I saw the light," or whatever, [for ghosts] it's kind of like a punishment in a way, most ghosts are, some of them are miserable, if you even believe in ghosts, I don't know.

Diamond clearly has a structured belief system about spirits and ghosts, though she would only reveal it if given the opportunity, as she did within this interview context. Even so, Diamond checked in with the interviewer to see if her beliefs were shared. In the con-text of the interview, the interviewer did not reveal her own beliefs, but instead acknowledged and validated Diamond's. It appeared as though that validation might be hard to come by, despite the fact that most people, like Diamond, do not see death as an end. Since most people hold this belief, or the possibility of this belief being true, the open-channel nature of mobile communication easily lends itself to becoming a tool to extend communication with loved ones beyond death. In the next section, we discuss exactly how elements of mobile communication could provide a foundation for unique uses of mobile media in times of grief.

THE OPEN-CHANNEL NATURE OF MOBILE COMMUNICATION

Mobile communication can be experienced as a source of continued interaction and as perpetual communication with loved ones that essentially never ends. Mobile communication does not require the formal openings and closings of more traditional forms of mediated communication. Because you are calling a person and not a place, mobile communication allows for direct person-to-person contact. Mobile devices can be used in ways that increase the intimacy produced between two people. People's personal information, not simply a phone number, is now stored in our devices.

Names and sometimes pictures associated with textual information can create an enduring link. These connections can be linked to social media sites and can generate a seamless merging between one-on-one communication and communication shared with others. For example, most text messaging platforms appear to be never-ending chains of communication between parties. Because of this, mobile phone users can quite easily envision their communication with those close to them to be ceaseless. Mobile communication is interconnected communication. Studies have shown the ways in which people easily transition from voice to text, and the ways in which there is no longer a need to recapitulate where a conversation left off in order to start a "new" one (Laursen 2013). There is always the opportunity for the conversation to resume at any point or time, with little to no effort or formality.

This perpetual connection with others can set the stage for people to believe in a mobile form of communication that does not end.

Even with the closing of a phone conversation, it is not uncommon to follow it up with a text, which Laursen (2013) calls a "resumption message." Resumption messages reopen a topic that may have been closed through the voice call. For example, a person may have a voice conversation with a partner on the phone in which he or she communicates that an agreed-upon meeting will take place, as scheduled, in fifteen minutes. The call ends with both parties saying goodbye. If, after hanging up, the partner texts the person to ask where he or she is now, that would be considered a resumption message. The conversation thread was closed via the voice call; the text messaging resumed the discussion.

Epilogue messages are also sent after a previous conversation was closed. In contrast to the resumption message, however, this message does not continue the conversation, but instead can be characterized as evaluative and a kind of meta-communication about the interaction that had taken place. It indicates that the previous conversation is still on the mind of the person sending the text. Epilogue messages may contain emotional content that reflects the disinhibited nature of mediated communication (Laursen 2013). For example, two people may have had an intimate conversation where there was an exchange of feelings. After the conversation is over, one of the conversation partners may text the other to indicate that she or he really enjoyed the conversation, or that the conversation has enhanced her or his feelings for the person. In this example, the epilogue message is not about resuming the conversation, but rather indicates the way in which the previous conversation is still alive within the person. Relating to this book's focus, these kinds of communication patterns indicate the ways in which mobile communication can be characterized as open and unrestricted, easily maintained and resumed, and capable of transcending the limitations of more formal or "real" forms of interaction, like that which is done face-to-face.

Conceptualized in this way, it does not seem difficult to imagine that some people would be able to use mobile devices and mobile media as a means to continue to be in conversation—connected—to their loved ones, regardless of whether they are alive or dead (as was depicted in the previous chapter, related to how some parents and loved ones responded to the loss of the children of the South Korean ferry disaster). In addition, it has been established that, throughout the grieving process, we develop creative ways of keeping the dead "alive" (Mitchell 2007). Focusing on this kind of mobile-emotive connection and the unique nature of mobile-mediated communication will guide this chapter as we explore mobile-emotive rituals of continuity.

MOBILE-EMOTIVE RITUALS OF CONTINUITY IN THE BEREAVEMENT PROCESS

Rituals of continuity reflect the continuation of bonds with those who have departed and the feelings of an ongoing relationship with those who are deceased (Wheeler-Roy and Amyot 2004). Through mobile-emotive rituals of continuity, the bereaved establish that lost loved ones are still a part of their life. As discussed in Section I, maintaining ties with loved ones even after they have departed is often a part of the grieving process. The bereaved maintain an attachment to the deceased. The presence of the dead in their lives comes through memories and daily reminders, which then trigger an emotional response that in the early days of grief can be quite intense, but then tends to diminish over time (Unruh 1983).

Mobile-emotive rituals of affirmation and intensification, as discussed in the previous section, all work to reinforce the bereaved person's emotional attachment to and identification with the deceased. The emotional labor of these rituals calls into question the strict divide between the living and the dead. Experiences that involve the exchange of affective material are the vehicles through which these affective bonds are continued (Valentine 2013). The mobile device then has the potential to become the medium through which forms of affective transmission can occur. The blurring of liveness and deadness can also be facilitated through the use of mobile media, since the device itself generates an ambiguity between what is happening in the here and now and what is projected or augmented by the presence of the device. Ultimately, the open nature of mobile communication and mobile media has the potential to fulfill the wish of continuing communication (in some form) with the deceased. The next section discusses the prevalence of after-death communication within the mourning process and the role that mobile media can play in generating "sense-of-presence experiences."

AFTER-DEATH COMMUNICATION VIA MOBILE MEDIA AS A CONTINUATION OF BONDS

After-death communication (ADC) is experienced by the bereaved as a means of continuing their bond with deceased loved ones. While not necessarily pathological or hallucinatory, Bill Guggenheim and Judy Guggenheim (1997) coined the term "after-death communication" to describe a spiritual and direct experience that occurs spontaneously and is experienced as contact with a deceased loved one, excluding those facilitated by a medium (Drewry 2003). ADC is experienced as spontaneous contact because it is interpreted by the bereaved as contact that was initiated by the deceased. ADC is intended to represent experiences in which a bereaved person appears to be "contacted" by a lost loved one, and is therefore "in communication" with that person. These encounters can generate a sense of the deceased loved one's presence through visual evidence, sounds, odors, dreams, or other kinds of synchronous events that the perceiver takes as a "message" from the loved one (Kwilecki 2011). Those that experience ADCs appear to be impacted emotionally and spiritually.

For the purposes of this book, the definition of ADC will be extended to represent the ways in which mobile media facilitate the phenomenological experiences that are then used by the bereaved to assist in their grief. It is not important to determine if these experiences are "real" or not, but rather to understand that in the mind of the bereaved, these experiences are significant and meaningful (Kalish and Reynolds 1973). In this way, these are apparent contacts not necessarily evidenced in ontological reality (Hastings 2012). And so, as was mentioned in the previous section, we are privileging the inner worlds of the individual as a means of acceptance of paranormal experiences. We function from the understanding that these kinds of experiences contribute to the meaning-making process of bereavement. In most cases, ADC is comforting and useful. In other cases, it can be disturbing and sometimes anxiety-provoking for the bereaved.

In order to understand the role that ADC plays in the grieving process, it is important to understand what happens after ADC is established. ADC often confirms or instills a belief in life after death. It often brings comfort and is a means of expressing the yearning to be reunited with the deceased loved one (Kwilecki 2011). And while the Guggenheims have documented the spontaneous nature of "contact," it is important to also understand that desire or fear of this contact may originate from the person experiencing it. He or she may first have a sense or desire that the deceased is still present, and then seek out ways of affirming and expressing that belief. ADC may start with the bereaved calling out or speaking out to the lost loved one. Most people understand that a loved one will not answer back, and they are often conscious of the suspension of disbelief they must create in order for the experience to feel "real" for them. Yet they engage in different forms of communication with their deceased loved ones as though they are listening or somehow still present.

After experiencing a loss, many people report feeling the presence of the person that has died. *Sense-of-presence experiences* are defined as "non-material quasi-sensory subjective but (experienced as) veridical feeling of presence of the deceased which tends to occur unexpectedly and is generally perceived as comforting, pleasant and helpful or positive" (Steffen and Coyle 2011, 580). The bereaved may also feel as though they are being watched over by their deceased loved ones (Bennett and Bennett 2000; Klugman 2006). Participants in the US study spoke of ways in which they acknowledged, through the use of their mobile media, that their deceased loved ones now functioned as their guardian angels (Doran and Downing Hansen 2006). Pamela (18, Caucasian, US) explained this as a way that she used the digital pictures stored on her device:

> I feel like sometimes she is watching over me, in a sense, kind of, but I know sometimes that I really have to let her go. I feel like when I am looking at her picture [on my phone], like I can talk to her or something. Like one moment she will pop up next to me or something.

Pamela discussed the ways in which she believes that her grandmother is still watching over her, that she senses her presence, especially when she looks at a digital picture of her grandmother on her phone. She struggled with the idea that her grandmother was remaining connected to her because Pamela still needed her. Pamela felt as though she needed to let her grandmother go, that the clinging and longing for her grandmother was what was keeping her grandmother bound to her. In this discussion, the interviewer was drawn into her belief and the emphatic way that she described the route she took to maintain her grandmother's presence via the coveting of digital photos. The interviewer asked Pamela to pull up one of the photos, and through this, Pamela's grandmother became a part of the interview. Pamela stated, "Because when I think about it, you know if I am looking at a picture long enough, I can remember being in her arms or something or like the way she used to smell." Pamela indicated that the picture helped her to conjure her connection to her grandmother, and by accessing the photo during the interview, it felt as though that experience became shared with the interviewer, and the mobile device itself functioned not unlike a psychomanteum.

With both ADC and sense-of-presence experiences, the bereaved desire to communicate with the deceased, to send them a message to let them know they are not forgotten. They also want confirmation from the dead that their spirits endure and they remain present. Social media, as accessed through one's mobile device, serves as a place for this form of expression and connection to happen. Laila (18, Hispanic/Latina, US) reported how she turned to social media as a venue to connect with her deceased mother. As with other US participants, the text of her posts addressed her mother directly—Laila provided this as evidence of her attempt at ADC, in combination with her reinterpretation of previously recorded digital material as a means of hearing her mother's voice beyond death. When asked about this, Laila responded,

> I felt like that because even though my mother wasn't connected to these things and wasn't Facebook-savvy or Instagram-savvy, she liked the concept of it, so I always felt—because she always liked getting her picture taken—I used to, I always used to think in my head [in a singsong voice], "Mom, you are becoming a celebrity!" I would really think that, every time I posted a picture of her. [Technology helps connect me to her] because she's still there, just for the fact that I am able to hear her voice. Like

something that gives me the possibility to do that is awesome. Even though if I don't remember it, I can still look back on it. And you know what? She's still there and I still remember it. And I feel so close to her when I am listening to a video or seeing me pause her. . . . It's awesome.

For Laila, who lost her mother at age seventeen, this form of connection and communication kept her mother a part of her everyday life and a part of her family. She discussed the ways in which she used her mobile device to generate these sense-of-presence experiences. When asked if she ever felt like she had a mystical or spiritual experience involving her mobile device, she responded,

Honestly, yeah, I guess—I think *mystical* I would choose, with the feeling of her being right there with me. Yeah, I felt one time I was watching this video—she was going to [her home country], because her sister had passed away. And we were making a video of her before she left. And then she was like, so she said in this video, and I still play it until this day, "I am going off to my country, so I will be gone for a little, but I'll be back!" I felt like she was right there with me. When she was like, "I'll be back," and when she says, "I love you all" [Laila starts to cry], and I was like, "I know." I feel like she'll be back . . . like she was right there, saying not to worry, that everything is going to be fine.

Laila's experience was emotionally powerful, raw, and real. She actively engaged her stored content to reveal the ways in which she could still feel in communication with her mother. Research on ADC has determined that most people experience this kind of continued bond as something that brings the bereaved a sense of emotional peace and comfort in the knowledge that the spirit of the deceased endures (Daggett 2005). Participants described how using mobile media in this way reassured them that their deceased loved ones were all right and still a presence in their life. Farah's (21, Arab/Orthodox Christian, US) experience represents a further example of the private and intimate space between the user and a device when feeling "in communication" with a deceased loved one. Farah believed that she was texting her deceased friend, and she struggled with the knowledge that she was actually sending text messages to a dead person. Yet she openly described how she suspended her disbelief in order to make it real. Throughout this segment of the interview, she struggled between representing the experience as something that really happened, on the one hand, and her thinking now that perhaps she made it up to distance herself from the reality of the loss, on the other:

> [She] is the [only] person that I felt OK to text, even after her death. Other than that, because in that year and a half [after her death], I used to talk to her like she was around. Like she is not gone yet, so I would text her, "Hi, how are you, what are we doing today?" Stuff like that. [I would text her] in the morning, in the afternoon, sometimes between the morning and the afternoon. [It started] after the forty days (significant in Arab Orthodox funereal tradition). So only her (the deceased), I would text, and not as often as we used to, *we* would text, uh, *I* would text, but not as often [as when she was alive]. (*Interviewer: Did you anticipate her responding?*) Yeah, all the time. I remember I texted her one time [after she died] about the joke we had, I used to call her [wild] and she would say [when she was alive], "Of course, I am [wild], that is what you love." One time I texted her that [after she died], "[Wild]?" And *she's* like, well *I* anticipated her, "Yeah of course I'm [wild], that is what you love." So I texted back, I said, "Of course that's what I love, how could I not love you!" Stuff like that. . . . I was having a conversation in my head and the texts were in the phone. . . . I mean for most of the times,

back then I could have sworn she was answering back. But now, I don't know, was she answering? Was she not answering?

Farah's struggle with her desire to continue her bond with her best friend beyond death and her acknowledgement that this might inhibit her ability to integrate the loss into her life, is something that many participants struggled with. When the interviewer asked her whether or not she believed that her friend was still with her, Farah stated,

> She can hear me! And I am sure she is praying for me up there. Right now, if I can imagine her telling me something, she will be like, "Honey, I am always going to be in your heart! But you need to move on and you need to let go." And I'll be like, "I can't let go of you! I can't, if I let go of you, I am letting go of most of myself."

What is remarkable here is that Farah was able to generate a private space that was only shared between her and her deceased loved one. The ongoing texts, as well as the ones she stored on her phone, facilitated a mobile-emotive psychomanteum and helped her make her continuing bond with her friend real. Farah described how difficult it was for her to then accidentally lose her phone, and thereby lose all the texts from her friend:

> I felt lost [after losing the phone]. Somehow, I used to share everything with her, whenever I had a problem, whenever I had anything, so those messages somehow felt like guiding me through even though she's not around. Like if I have a problem, or a similar situation that happened earlier, I would go back and see what she told me. See what her advice was, see if it goes with the situation or not.

Farah experienced losing her phone as though she lost her friend again. It was the device itself that held her friend's spirit, and no other mobile media or social media connection was as powerful. Similar to other participants, Farah rejected the use of social media to honor or connect with her deceased loved one. She never posted anything to Facebook or Instagram regarding the loss. Again, it could be that she wanted to remain in the unreality of the loss. For most participants, posting to social media meant acknowledging that the loved one had passed. Farah did not have the desire to do that. Even in her mentioning that maybe some people have forgotten her friend, she wanted to emphasize that she did not forget. To others, Farah's friend was dead and ceased to exist; in Farah's mobile-emotive psychomanteum, via her mobile device, she was still alive:

At that time [of her death], I wasn't on Facebook all that much. My phone was really only for texting *her*. I feel like this stuff is mine. There, and not sharable with everyone. I feel like, maybe everyone forgot about her but I didn't. I can't.

While Farah preferred the private and intimate nature of her mobile device to generate her sense of connection, other participants explained how social media posts could also be used to produce sense of presence experiences and ADC. US participant Gina (18, Caucasian) shared such an experience:

Sometimes I just say how much I miss him or how he looked so happy here and stuff like that. . . . I have it here, like I can show you [pauses to find post]. Here I have the picture, and I have the words here [reading post]: "This past month made me realize how much I miss you and how hard everything is without you, hopefully you're resting peacefully. *(Interviewer: And then you have #love you, #grandpa, #one, #only, . . .)* When I write things like that I feel like he's listening, and that he knows how I'm feeling and maybe because he'd rather me just say how I feel rather than just not say anything at all. At least it's him knowing that, like I'm saying that out loud, in general, he knows how I'm dealing with it [his passing].

Gina also mentioned how she preferred connecting with her grandfather via social media rather than in any other way. She discussed how face-to-face conversations and reminiscing with family was not as impactful as the intimate space she could generate through her social media posts. For the US participants, social media functioned as a preferred venue for rituals of continuity that involve writing directly to the deceased. They had an awareness that, in all likelihood, their deceased loved ones were not reading their social media posts. They often put that knowledge aside to engage in this narrative process that seemed to help them understand their loss better. Social media's ability to not be bound by time and space allowed for the bereaved to experience a sense of freedom of expression of their emotional concerns, without the fear of placing a burden on friends and family. This was often the motive behind creating memorial pages on Facebook. Chantal (19, Jamaican, US) explained this regarding the memorial page that was established for her boyfriend after he was murdered:

Even though I'm not necessarily talking to him it makes me feel as though I am—when you write directly on the page, when you phrase it directly towards him. It's not like you are commenting to other people—you're sending a message directly to him, like, "Thank you for what you have done," or "You helped me with this and this situation," or jokes that they have or memories. People would write those type of things. (*Interviewer: Does it help you with the loss?*) In a little way, I guess, 'cause I am talking to him, 'cause I don't really talk about him to my sisters anymore because

I don't want to constantly talk about it to family members and stuff, so yeah. I don't talk about it to anyone anymore.

Similar to Gina, Chantal preferred using social media as her point of access to her deceased loved one. She was also comforted in the knowledge of the Facebook page's existence, that it was always there and that she could access it at any time as a means of accessing her deceased boyfriend's presence. Posting to social media as a means of ADC was viewed as comparable to other extrasensory experiences with the dead, like those experienced through dreaming. This comparison may indicate that, for some, social/mobile media space and the more private "space" of the individual's mobile device could be conceived of, as mentioned previously, as a liminal space not fully connected to ontological reality, in which you have a sense that what is happening is not "real," but that you can participate in this realm of unreality in the same way that you may participate in a dream state. Some US participants characterized social media as an ideal way to continue their bond with lost loved ones, and some felt regret after a death if the loved one did not have a Facebook presence prior to death. As Pamela (18, Caucasian) noted,

[If my grandma somehow had a Facebook page] I think I would go back and try to keep talking to her. Or something. [When people "talk" to their loved ones through their Facebook pages] I think in their heart they know that they are not going to get an answer, but I think it just brings them back to like, "Maybe if I just write on their wall, they *will* answer," or they [the deceased] are seeing it in some way.

In the previous examples, participants had some belief in literal immortality. They believed that their loved ones' spirits still existed beyond death. Beliefs in symbolic immortality were reflected in the ways in which people utilized some memorialization practices via mobile media. While there is some overlap here with posting to social media as a means of generating a sense of co-present companionship with the dead, in the bereavement and memorialization process, honoring a person's death anniversary and birthday, in the US context, was also a way to keep the deceased loved one's memory alive, and to do what was right for the dead. Participants struggled with trying to find a justification or motivation for postings directed at the deceased, as in this exchange with Olivia (19, American, with diverse ethnic background):

> (*Interviewer: But did you always use that tone where you felt like you were writing, as though you were talking directly to her?*) Yeah, I did, actually, . . . yeah. I don't know I guess. . . . Like now I would probably say, "*She* was," . . . but at the time it was, "*You* are an amazing," . . . I don't know . . . it is actually kind of weird, I don't know why I did that. It wasn't like I thought she was going to see it or anything. I guess I don't know.

As Olivia grappled with trying to understand why she posted the way that she did, she recognized that, with time, her motivation and her method of posting changed as her relationship to the loss changed. There did appear, in the US examples, to be some trajectory related to these experiences in which the desire for connection and communication with the deceased was usually stronger during the earlier, more acute phases of grief. Yet the postings persisted well into the grieving process. Participants' struggles with continuing bonds with the deceased seemed to arise only out of felt social pressure to conform to some expected resolution related to the grief process. As discussed in a previous chapter, the social expectation in the US context, which relates to traditional psychological grief models, is that grief should find some end, some resolution, and that, ultimately, the bond will cease.

CONCLUSION: MOBILE-EMOTIVE REANIMATION

Part of the consequence of ADC and sense-of-presence experiences is that the deceased become reanimated. As we described with the *Sewol* case study, and as was demonstrated in this chapter in the ways that other people participate in keeping shared loved ones "alive" through technology use, mobile media can facilitate a reanimation process that allows for the bereaved to re-establish a connection to the dead. Through the use of mobile media, the dead maintain a presence, whether symbolic or literal, in the lives of their loved ones, and, in essence, their loved ones provide a space that could be considered an extension of the deceased's afterlife. The notion of "going viral" takes on a deeper significance here in that social media postings about a person and remembering them become a way of perpetuating their existence beyond physical death.

Prior to engagement through social media and text-based chat applications, conversation about the dead most often happened on a one-to-one basis. While it is comforting and intimate, perpetuating the presence of the deceased via these conversations does not have the same impact as the experience of calling a loved one to mind via a social media post. Because of the co-creative nature of social media, in a matter of minutes, based on one post about the deceased, ten or twenty people could be thinking about them, and in turn maybe share a memory of their own, and in an instant the deceased's presence is symbolically reanimated! This kind of symbolic reanimation is closely related to the definition of symbolic immortality, in that long after the loved one is gone, digital remains can be preserved, shared, and perpetuated. How social and mobile media content is stored on the device itself can extend our lives electronically.

Although the bereaved struggle at times with sharing these experiences, they appear to also play an important role in the sense-making aspect of the grief process (Valentine 2008). ADC experiences may help the bereaved in understanding the loss and in finding some solace in getting a form of acknowledgment that their loved one is okay in death (Sanger 2009). However, it should also be noted here that not everyone is engaged in using the technology in this way. Many of our participants were not comfortable with this aspect of the use of social and mobile media. In our concluding chapter, we revisit the major themes of this book and highlight next steps for exploring mobile-emotive rituals of use and their relationship to grief and loss.

8

Conclusion

Mobilizing Death

Heaven
It will be the past
and we'll live there together.

Not as it was to live
but as it is remembered.

It will be the past.
We'll all go back together.

Everyone we ever loved,
and lost, and must remember.

It will be the past.
And it will last forever.

—Patrick Phillips, from *Boy* (2008), reprinted with permission from
The University of Georgia Press.

When Soo-hyun lost her brother in the *Sewol* disaster, it was his mobile device that became a repository for memories of him as well as a transitory object with which Soo-hyun could negotiate her continuing bonds with her now-deceased brother. Over in Manila, when

Valentina lost her mother to cancer after months of being by her side, it was the mobile phone that became the vehicle for her mother's spirit. From the visuality akin to photo albums, to the textuality of old text messages, to the recorded voice messages, the mobile phone allowed Valentina to keep reliving her relationship with her mother.

As the poem, "Heaven" (2008) by Patrick Phillips describes, some bereaved have the potential to generate a constructed sense of heaven in their minds. For some, the promise of reunion is the promise of "heaven." For others, there is reincarnation. For still others, the complexity of beyond the Anthropocene (that is, a period marked by the human damage of the environment) is unimaginable. Through mobile-emotive devices, users have the imaginative ability to extend their consciousness and, in essence, extend their ability to make heaven real. Regardless of one's belief in an afterlife, the cultivation, maintenance, and enactment of mobile-emotive archives allows for us to revisit a past that has the potential to live forever.

Throughout the chapters in this book, we see how mobile devices are both expanding upon older forms of memory-making and creating new channels for affective cultures whereby the visual, textual, oral, and haptic manifest in new ways. Encompassing everything from phones to tablets, mobile media are playing a key role not only in how we represent and remember life, but also in how we negotiate the increasingly integral role of the digital within rituals in and around death. Mobile media highlight the role of death rituals as a perpetual tension between traditional practices and social change. Rather than transforming ritualization, there is an oscillation between media shaping and being shaped by existing ritualistic behaviors. As a pivotal part of everyday life, mobile media are essential in the narrative approach to making sense of grief, as well as in providing a liminal space in which to negotiate the continuation of bonds and to manage the emotionality of events pertaining to loss. Throughout this book, we have attempted to define the texture of mobile-emotive grief and mourning in and around mobile media use. We have argued that during times of distress, mobile media can assist, accompany, and at times augment the disruptive terrain of loss.

Mobile media magnify inner subjectivities while simultaneously reinforcing existing rituals and expanding upon new types of relationships (Pertierra 2006). We have explored here the particular affordances of mobile media in the negotiation of tradition amid social change and paradigm shifts. Through mobile media memorialization, we see changing notions of what it means to be alive and the ways in which the integration of mobile media is changing our perspectives on deadness and the afterlife.

By drawing upon ethnographic and comparative methods, we have outlined some of the diverse and yet common themes manifesting at both an individual and cultural level around bereavement, as well as the ongoing relations between the living and the dead. Examining death rituals allows for a rethinking and reassessment of core values in a society. Many cultures believe in an afterlife and demonstrate it through different rituals. In most cultures, death is a highly emotional and sometimes taboo subject, making it very hard to study. In Western cultures in particular, death and mourning, while often ritualized through religious tradition, are still viewed as a highly private activity whereby entering a mourner's space could be deemed intrusive.

And yet, as social and mobile media and SNS such as Facebook, LINE (Japan), Twitter, WeChat, and Kakao become a significant part of everyday life, so too do the boundaries between the intimate and public, the private and the social, become entangled in new ways. As much of the literature on digital memorialization demonstrates, death and dying are embedded within the fabric of the online. The digital is extending earlier memorial practices such as photography (postmortem as well as portrait), and also creating new ways in which death and loss manifest within our daily lives (Gibbs et al.

2015; Brubaker et al. 2012; Graham et al. 2013; Lingel 2013; Church 2013; Deger 2008, 2006).

Haunting Hands expands upon debates in the area of online memorialization (Gibbs et al. 2015a; Brubaker et al. 2012), whereby new media are seen to enable people's lives to be expanded, witnessed, and recontextualized, in a multiplicity of ways (Graham et al. 2013, 133). While the fact that digital data allow new forms in which to construct life, death, and after-death is unquestionable (Marwick and Ellison 2012; Brubaker and Hayes 2011; Brubaker et al. 2012; Bollmer 2013, 2015), nuanced studies into the specific affordances of particular media, cultural contexts, and the role of visual UCC is required.

There is a need to put the "digital" in *context* with older analog and cultural processes to fully understand the role of the digital in the rituals, representations, and relationships in and around life, loss, and death in the everyday. Or, as Refslund Christensen and Gotved (2015) have argued, it is important to understand the tapestry that is mediation, remediation, and mediatization. In this book, we have demonstrated that the mobile device itself becomes essential during times of distress because of its communicative or social function, but also because of the ways in which it can both contain and generate an intimate space within it. In this way, the device becomes an important companion for mobile-emotive grief as the bereaved engage with emotionally charged digital content in solitary, sometimes secretive, and sometimes shared ways.

We have recognized the importance of contextualizing mobile media within broader historical rituals around grief and loss. While photography has always had a complicated relationship with power, representation, and death (Barthes 1981; Sontag 1977; Deger 2008), the social life of the digital is changing the relationship between memory, image ownership (Brubaker 2016), witnessing (Papailias 2016), and dissemination (Stanyek and Piekut 2010). The increasingly prevalent role of the digital after death means that death and after-life are becoming more quotidian and yet intimately public (Graham et al. 2013). These extensions of life and afterlife (in death) are amplified by mobile media as a practice fully embedded within the everyday (Goggin 2006). In this book, we have explored some of the implications of the array of mobile media now embedded within rituals of grief and loss.

In this concluding chapter, we seek to provide a set of propositions for future areas of study. We emphasize that these emergent practices are a constant negotiation of tradition and social change, and that mobile-emotive content is increasingly becoming an essential part of the rituals around grief, whereby there is a mobile-mediated co-presence (between the bereaved and their communities of support) and the continuation of bonds (between life and after-life). Mobile media has many manifestations—from the immaterial, digital, and inorganic to the material and symbolic—that enliven the dead through its use and nonuse. What follows is an exploration of future propositions to extend this work.

TESTING THE LIMIT(LESS): SELFIES AT FUNERALS

From the increased role of camera phones in documenting disaster and tragedy, to the self-memorialization processes of the soon-to-be-deceased, to the recapturing of the deceased after death, mobile media are impacting how we experience and represent loss. Loss is being rendered as both *intimate* and *public* in new ways through mobile media (Hjorth and Arnold 2013; Goggin 2011; McQuire 2008; Stevens 2009). In Bjorn Nansen et al.'s (2014) work, the role of selfies at funerals is explored. Here we see that selfies are testing the limits of Western rituals around grief as a private process. The selfie is not just a barometer for today's so-called narcissistic, networked, infinite regress; rather, it draws upon various traditions, including artistic, media, technological, generational, emotional, and cultural cartographies.

As Brooke Wendt notes in *The Allure of the Selfie* (2014), challenging McLuhan, the narcissism of the selfie is not about self-love but about a numbness and misrecognition. Following this argument, our millions of selfies are about an infinite regress of misrecognition or a numbness to the present. In this, the mobile device mediates the emotionality of the event and provides a dualistic vehicle for coinciding psychological closeness *and* psychological distance, depending on the contextualizing and decontextualizing of the digital object. The most defining moment related to funeral selfies happened when President Barack Obama took the now infamous selfie at Nelson Mandela's funeral (December 10, 2013), with the Danish and the British prime ministers. In this event, tacit etiquette about what was an appropriate selfie setting had been transgressed.

Despite President Obama's obvious attempt to celebrate the life of Mandela through the selfie, and to represent, perhaps, the vast gathering of dignitaries at the event, his seeming irreverence related to the memorial service moved the genre of the funeral selfie into a new place from which there was no return. The production of selfies within private spaces, such as the funeral, presents the penultimate definition of how our limits between what is intimate and what is public are now being negotiated by, and through, mobile media. The fact that selfies at funerals are now rather commonplace is part of the shift occurring in invisible and visible practices in mourning sociality.

In the *Sewol* disaster, we saw how selfies are no longer one mere genre, but rather are a complex field for variety of modes of affects and witnessing. Through the selfie-as-eulogy, we saw different gradiations in terms of apperception—some knew the photographing would be there last, in that way, playing to a very Barthesian sense of photographers as "agents of death," whereby, through the act of photographing the subject becomes a specter (Barthes 1981, 92). Increasingly, selfies are used as part of visualizing notions of recovering (Hendry 2016), and as a part of an individual's self-eulogizing process. With the uptake of mobile media across generations (with many grandparents desiring mobile media literacy in order to engage with their grandchildren), we see how mobile media increasingly play a role in how one engages with the dying process—including playing a role in the construction of one's own eulogy. We saw an example of this in the case of the *Sewol* disaster, in which school children used camera phones to film the disaster and to capture their parting words to their loved ones. We also saw how notions of death and grieving differ, subject to cultural context.

As Papailias (2016) notes in the case of YouTube as "affective network," networked media create a type of sociality around mourning and witnessing. Through the comments section in YouTube, witnessing texts can be formed as part of what she calls an "intersubjective sphere of mourning" (8). The comments are embodied and create a sense of "bodily intimacy and spatial copresence" through gesturing and linguistic acts such as "shuddering, trembling, stomach tightening, crying, and weeping" (8). For Papailias, viral memorials are interwoven with "affective public in the assemblage of mourning" (1). The selfie-as-eulogy genre can be as much intentional as unintentional. Around September 2015, a slate of short articles were published identifying that "selfie deaths are now more common than shark attacks" (Lewis 2015; Horton 2015). Behind this tagline were examples of selfie accidents, including an elderly Japanese tourist falling down a set of stairs to his death after attempting a selfie, and young men run down by a train while trying to get selfies. All the articles showcased the Russian selfie guide (see Figure 8.1) as a model for avoiding accidental selfie-as-eulogies.

In Western cultures, much time and energy is given over to celebrating the beginning of life. Facebook feeds are full of cute babies

Figure 8.1 Russian signs to avoid dangerous selfies.

(alongside cute pets). In contrast, the end of life has tended to be noted by absence, by the *lack* of camera phone images, Facebook feeds, shared stories. Yet as more and more people, both young and old, become new-media literate through mobile media, stories of dying, death, and the dead are becoming more prevalent. Increasingly, spaces like social and mobile media are becoming spaces to celebrate and reflect upon life not only at the beginning, but also at the end. Just as the 2015 Facebook debate about *emojis* and the introduction of a "dislike" button highlighted, we need more ways and methods to celebrate life, death, and after-death beyond simplified social media affirmation.

Increasingly, new ways for reflecting upon death are emerging through mobile media. Some methods, like "selfies at funerals," have been deemed inappropriate by many, while other methods, like the selfies in the Korean ferry and amid tragedy, may have helped to further bond and unite families in crisis and publics in mourning in ways that are both *intimate* and *public*. The role that mobile media play in the wake of disasters and other tragedies is something that we only touched upon in this book; increasingly as the debates around the Anthropocene point to progressively more disasters in the future, further research will be needed. In the next section, we explore the relationship between disasters, grief, and mobile media.

COMPARING DISASTERS, GRIEF, AND MOBILE MEDIA

As we have demonstrated through examples such as the *Sewol* disaster and Japan's 3/11 tragedy, mobile media are playing a key role in the documentation and affect/effect of disasters globally. We have deployed micro and macro examples of mobile media memorialization, from disasters to personal loss. The significance of mobile media in disasters has begun to gain traction in media studies (Hjorth and Kim 2011a, 2011b) especially around mobile media platforms like Twitter (Bruns et al. 2012). Unlike platform studies that focus on the affordances of a specific platform such as Facebook or Twitter, by taking a mobile media approach, we consider a more nuanced model of how death and loss is navigated in and around everyday life.

Just as death and mourning are culturally specific, so too are the practices in and around mobile media. Each cultural context has different technological and socioeconomic issues that inform mobile media practices. For example, Tokyo is home to frequent typhoons and earthquakes, so governments, industry, and individuals have utilized mobile media in crisis management planning. In Tokyo, especially since the aforementioned events of March 2011 (3/11), one can find mobile phone (*keitai*) apps for earthquake procedures implemented by the government. In the chaotic hours and days after disastrous events, mobile media have come to play a key role, both literally and symbolically (Hjorth and Kim 2011b; Gill, Steger, and Slater 2013). Mobile media have also played a pivotal role in the recent uprising against government policies in Japan, a country where public protest is not the norm (Gill, Steger, and Slater 2013).

In Western contexts like the United States or Australia, the rapid uptake of smartphones over the last couple of years has seen a migration of the digital and online from predominantly stationary personal computers to mobile media. The migration from the stationary to the mobile has informed the types of content, genres, and contexts in which mobile media is generated and shared. As we have argued in this book, mobile media afford a particular type of affect that shapes, and is shaped by, cultural rituals. As mentioned earlier, Ahmed (2004) views emotions as not just psychological and individuated, but also as an embedded part of cultural practices. She points to the relationship between emotions, language, and bodies as the playground for processes of affect. For Ahmed, emotions are as political as they are social. She also argues that affect is that which "sticks"—to people, places, and objects (2010, 29). Taking this reading of emotion and affect, we can see that mobile media memorialization processes can highlight not just micro but also macro relations.

As we have argued, the emotions in and around mobile media do create a particular tool kit of affects that are different from stationary digital media. For example, the "personal, pedestrian, and portable" (Ito et al. 2005) characteristics of mobile media mean that they have a specific relationship to the body and intimacy (Fortunati 2002; Lasèn 2004). We can define these phenomena in terms of the mobile-emotive co-presence and rituals.

Future studies into this area will not only need to negotiate these particular mobile-emotive forms of co-presence and ritual in terms of tradition versus social change, but also in relation to more longitudinal comparative research. If we are truly to understand the relationship between death and the rituals of grief we need to monitor these cycles beyond the older Western "limits" of the funeral. For example, how does mobile media help people deal with their bereavement processes a decade after they have lost a loved one? Moreover, there will be a need to interrogate the role of data and its haunting as digital traces of ourselves increasingly grow. Once upon a time, the family of the deceased would have had to deal with the material traces left behind—the clothes, the house, the books, the printed photographs, and so on. With the material increasingly becoming entangled with the immaterial, the closing down of online accounts and the limiting of digital traces will become harder to control. How will the impact of "big data" shape how mobile media memorialization plays out? For example, what happens to all the qualified self-data of the deceased? And what stories does this data tell? How will this phenomenon impact the role of "stewarding" by loved ones of the deceased? In the next section we further our arguments around the role that mobile-emotive rituals serve in assisting the bereaved in the processes of reconstructing their lives beyond loss.

A NEW KIND OF PUBLIC MOURNING: MOBILE-EMOTIVE RECONSTRUCTION AND RESILIENCE

While sometimes unintentional, the saturation of images and information shared through social media and other mobile media platforms literally places death directly in our faces. We now have the experience of having access (whether we want it or not) to uncensored and unflinching faces of death through the intimate publics of social media. People can use these documentaries in a forensic or diarized way to provide evidence and to reconstruct what has occurred. Mobile media applications are increasingly being used not just to quantify our lives, but also to record and archive our existence.

However, the digital nature of the evidence allows it to be edited and used to perpetuate the "life" and the "death" of the subject.

As we saw through the case studies and interviews, there is often now a demand placed on mobile media users to grieve in public. More than just the desire to bear witness, social media provides a space where others can participate in an individual's grief, thereby making all grief communal and all mourning "shared." Similar to other advancements in communication technology, the extensive use of mobile devices may have sparked an electric retribalization of modern society (Davis 1998). Public communal grief emerges as we join others through visual and textual material shared via our devices. As these rituals extend to social media, the role of commenting on people's social media posts serves as a reminder of the ways in which we participate in a seemingly larger social circle beyond those with whom we are face-to-face.

Despite the potential for spectacle, mobile-emotive co-presence and rituals enacted during periods of distress ameliorate the suffering of loss. Yet the less intimate social media spaces generated through its use may not be viewed as places of sincere exchange. Sincerity may still need to be authenticated, and loss experiences validated, through face-to-face interaction and perhaps also through mobile-to-mobile contact. There are no hard and fast rules about whether or not mobile-mediated connection to others is less intimate or sincere than other forms of communication. The ambiguous nature of mobile communication leaves this open to interpretation. For some users, social and mobile media intensifies connection between individuals. Yet for other users, engaging social and mobile media serves to distance them from the emotionality of the experience of grief (Gibbs et al. 2015a).

The documenting of the grief processes in and through mobile media challenges what is deemed natural. It also highlights the ways in which grief is constructed differently across generational, gendered, and cultural divides. The capacity for mobile media to make public, and even viral, intimate feelings of grief has yet to be analyzed fully as they play out globally in public discourses. Here we see the need for more research into the uncontrollable nature of digital content and how it plays against more traditional, Western ideas of grief.

Resilience is defined as the capacity to recover quickly from traumatic experiences. While there may be less emphasis on letting go as part of the trajectory of the mourning process, resilience is still an expected outcome. There is a difference between "letting go" and "getting over it." Users narrated the ways in which mobile-emotive resilience could be demonstrated through shifts in the ways they used their devices and social media to get back to "normal." This shift was often performed among rituals employed to keep lost loved ones "alive" in their imagination. In essence, mobile devices assist users to allow the loss to become integrated into the everyday, yet they also provide the means through which a bond with a lost loved one endures. Routinization and automaticity of use may function as a means through which the bereaved return to the living and compartmentalize their grief. This does not eliminate the potential for users to engage with mobile-emotive content in more isolated moments. In the next section, we discuss how mobile-emotive companionship could be focused solely on times when we are alone with our devices.

IN MEMORY OF ALONE TIME: MY DEVICE AND ME

> Martha [on mobile with dead husband's avatar]: I think I am going mad.
> Ash [dead husband as mobile phone avatar]: I won't tell anyone, if you don't.
> —*Black Mirror,* Season 2, Episode 1, "Be Right Back" (2013)

As was evidenced through the case studies and interviews, mobile media users' relationship with their devices resulted from a cultivated sense of dependency and attachment. Within psychological literature, the alignment between loneliness and digital media has been a site for contestation (see Sherry Turkle), and its roots in the connection versus disconnection debate can be found throughout media. The relationship between social networking sites (SNS) and loneliness has not been easy to understand (Saggaf and Nielsen 2014). As with other attempts to understand the relationship between psychological characteristics and mobile-mediated or computer-mediated behavior, it becomes a chicken-or-egg type of question: are lonely people more vulnerable to becoming attached or dependent on their connections through social and mobile media, or does social and mobile media make people feel lonely?

As Judy Wajcman (2015) has identified, technologies occupy a paradoxical relationship in our lives—they are blamed for the speeding up of time, and they are seen as solving the problems around acceleration. However, while "time"—and especially acceleration—has become a key preoccupation of our period, it needs to be understood in terms of broader class and cultural patterns around progress. For example, someone's privileged need for acceleration often comes at the cost of someone else's enforced slowness (e.g., taxi drivers waiting in New York for rich passengers who have a sense of urgency). And while there are debates around the future of automation and artificial intelligence (AI) about changing labor practices, slowness is still the required modality for care in and around loss and grief. It is these differing temporalities in, and around, mourning and media that will need to be accounted for. Grief cannot be accelerated. It also often involves symbolism that doesn't align with social media's focus upon the visual. Like previous technologies, mobile media shapes, and is shaped by, our rituals and practices. Through the media, new forms of expectation and etiquette are negotiated.

In our fieldwork, discussing mobile-emotive contexts underscored the emotional attachment that many users have towards their devices. What was particular to our findings was that as mobile devices expand in functionality, the specificities of contact become less important than the more general feelings that they provide of mobile-emotive companionship. Before mobile devices had ready access to social media and the Internet, users needed to identify specific people to contact in order to feel connected. It may be that with the ability to access SNS and other forms of mobile media via individual mobile devices, the *feeling* of connectedness may be experienced more frequently than face-to-face connection. Could it be that the continual bond we feel with, and through, our devices carries as much psychological weight as the bond we feel with those to whom we give face time? These issues continue to pose methodological challenges for mobile communication studies. For it is only through the study of these extended domains of social interaction, in conjunction with each other and not as separate spheres, that we can begin to understand how the integration of mobile devices into our everyday is impacting our understanding of relationships, social expectations and significant life events (Cumiskey and Ling 2015).

The imprints that our mobile devices leave on us are enduring. Like photographs, they haunt us. As Barthes (1981) noted in the case of photographs, they capture death and its specters. Mobile media, as devices intrinsically entangled within so many people's lives, are thus also the vessels for, and of, haunting. The ambiguity and multiplicity of its co-present nature across various temporal, spatial, and psychological realms means that the mobile is the perfect vehicle for witnessing, and being witness to, our mobile-emotive lives. The devices do become extensions of ourselves—through them, with them, and in them we cultivate a dualistic presence—one that is lived within and alongside the digital. As we have established, the power of the mobile lies in its capacity to house our experiences in intimate and yet co-present ways.

Being alone with our devices while simultaneously feeling connected to others demonstrates a hybrid co-presence, in which social media users may conceive of their "friends" or followers as an ever-present, intimate and familiar, yet also amorphous group. When broadcasting or posting something, they may be addressing the social media platform as their point of contact and connection, while not contacting anyone in particular. In this, there is a tacit acknowledgment that they are, in fact, alone, but are still companioned by an often-silent group of known others. Take, for example, the immediate aftermath of the police killing of Philando Castile, which was broadcast live on Facebook on July 6, 2016, via his girlfriend Diamond "Lavish" Reynolds' mobile phone. Diamond, upon being detained and handcuffed by police, said, "They threw my phone, Facebook." In addressing all those that she is connected with—through Facebook and those who were watching the scene unfold live—she imagined a type of collective witnessing and companionship as "Facebook," not as any particular individual. Together as "Facebook," those watching—some of whom were friends and family, later to become viewed by others over 5.7 million times—provided companionship for her and her daughter through what was most likely the worst day of their lives. The presence of the phone as "Facebook" interlocutor provided a particular channel and context for her grief. Her ongoing prayer—alongside her broadcasting the details of the event to her viewers—may have literally served as a lifeline for her. As the psychologist Jim Hopper observed, "She's grasping for dear life to these phrases, to this phone. You can think of it as a life raft to try to get through this" (Paquette 2016).

Mobile media may become a psychological lifeline for us. We hope that mobile media can come to rescue us in our most desperate hours and in the times when we don't want to be alone. In this, and without much doing, mobile media then become us. With a device as a constant companion, we can fantasize that we are never truly alone. This desire to not be left behind or forgotten about can be intimately tied to the ways in which we hope that we carry on beyond physical death. Through our ongoing, never-ceasing use of mobile media, we leave behind a digital self that has the potential to live on without us. In the next section we discuss these mobile-emotive legacies and the challenges of digital memorialization.

MOBILE-EMOTIVE LEGACIES: TRACES OF THE DIGITAL SELF WE LEAVE BEHIND

Is there anything wrong with creating a space where some aspect of ourselves will never end, so that those living may stay attached to our digital relics and view them as a blessing, as a source of protection, connection, and continual bond? What is the trouble with a love that never ends, with a self that never ends and that can continue beyond our active participation? (Steinhart 2014). What remains digitally beyond our physical death is reliant upon how much we have invested in creating a digital "self" while alive. This active construction of a digital self, in essence, creates a fiction, a digital trace of our actual selves. The process of memorialization via co-present others further distorts any version of "us." What is kept and what is thrown away is even more out of our hands with the tyranny of the digital after we die.

A viable continuation of the self in the virtual domain is about identity preservation. Strategies for identity preservation include activities that the dying and the grieving employ to "keep certain identities intact and alive for the future" (Unruh 1983, 341). This often involves the process of reminiscence. We found that the mobile-emotive continuation of a digital self typically involves using digital content to remember and retell stories of lost loved ones. Social media platforms allow for access to digital photos and older shared content. Repurposing these ordinary online posts can serve to shape the legacy that users leave behind. Coveting the digital devices of the dead can also serve as a means of preserving the identity of the deceased.

Unlike social media, there is a perception that devices of individuals are more private in nature (unless hacked). Many people now include in their estate planning how they want to be remembered online and with whom they wish to leave their mobile devices. The legal debates surrounding these issues and the ensuing legislation provide glimpses into how a person's digital legacy occupies our imagination and the significant role it plays in providing insight into who the person was when alive (Carroll and Romano 2011).

With the rise in digital memorialization (Nansen et al. 2014) through mobile media, new forms of etiquette around death are emerging. This has attracted debate about whether Facebook profiles of the dead should be allocated to special contexts. Some argue that the haunting of the deceased in everyday life through Facebook pages on the mobile phone adequately reflects how we may be in less control of this legacy than we think (Gibson 2014). With the worldwide proliferation of Facebook users, it is only natural that Facebook profiles will become "digital grave markers scattered amongst the profiles of the living" (Kasket 2012, 250). However, just as with real grave markers, what, if anything, continues to exist beyond the Facebook grave? Despite the ways in which mobile media blur the boundaries between the online and the offline, there may be ways in which the online can still provide a space apart and separated from offline contexts within which memorialization and veneration can occur. Future research needs to investigate these contexts of mourning separately, along with the ways in which they cannot be pulled apart.

As has been our focus in this book, localized media and mobile-mediated sites both extend traditional rituals and generate new ones. The relationship between life and death online and offline has been explored in game studies. The virtual worlds of social media and Massively Multiplayer Online Games (MMOGs or MMOs) such as

The *World of Warcraft* (*WoW*) have a long history of holding funerals and wakes for players—sometimes when the player dies online, but also when the player dies offline. It is important to see the online and offline as entangled and thus never truly separate, but rather interrelated.

One of the key events in game history was the *Serenity Now WoW* gatecrash in which hundreds of avatars paid their respects to a player who had died in real life, only to be gatecrashed by other players who tried to kill them. On March 4, 2006, friends of the player Fayejin, who had died of a stroke in real life, had planned to meet at the Frostfire Hot Springs in Winterspring (this destination was, of course, within the game online—on the game's PvP servers). This "place" was picked because she loved to fish (within the game) and loved the snow. This plan was posted to one of the game's message boards. The planners of this event had intended to create a digital recording of it to then share with Fayejin's offline family, and so they requested that players respect the intention of the funeral. This request was not honored when, during the course of the service, some players of the Once Alliance, Serenity Now guild chose to bust into it and pillage and murder players in attendance at the solemn online event.

The carnage of the gatecrash was then posted on YouTube for all to see. Here we see the power of witnessing and its affect (Papailias 2016). Even in the context of a "game," social expectations about respecting the domain of the funeral were challenged by the move of some players to exploit it. The incident was debated in the gaming community, with many agreeing that what the gatecrashers did was unethical.[1] Players who were impacted by the gatecrash wrote on message boards seeking revenge for the violation. These revenge fantasies posted online included violating the funerals of offending

1. http://www.youtube.com/watch?v=IHJVolaC8pw; this video depicts the gatecrash and has over six million views.

players' loved ones offline. This incident demonstrates the emotional world of the online and the ways in which individual users may, alone or collectively, invest in using that space in similar ways that other "real life" spaces may be used in the process of memorialization and funereal rites.

Participants in MMO game worlds also engage in virtual veneration by creating ancestor veneration avatars (AVA) as a means through which they can continue their bond with loved ones who have passed on. Through AVAs, online gamers can virtually embody the characteristics of a deceased loved one. These avatars can work to create a deeply psychological and emotional space that, with the suspension of disbelief, can lead one to feeling as though these characters can die, be resurrected, be recreated, and live once more (Bainbridge 2013). Virtual avatars of the deceased are inspiring development within the field of artificial intelligence (AI).

In attempts to recreate and regenerate the personality, intelligence, and creativity of the deceased, being able to maintain and build upon an ancestor avatar may be a means through which the impact sustained by the loss can be diminished. The potential for the consciousness of a person to be extended beyond physical death means that some aspects of a person may, in fact, become immortal (See Philip K. Dick Android Project for an example of this, at http://www.pkdandroid.org/robotic-portrait.htm). Of course, the promise of the eternal that data provide is not guaranteed, and our digital selves may still be vulnerable to deletion, to getting lost, to a digital death (for example, the Philip K. Dick Android Project was thwarted because his "head" was left behind on a plane).

Contained within the online, the contributions we have made via content become sites through which others can participate in honoring our memory as well. When the Scottish filmmaker Ryan McHenry died of bone cancer, the Hollywood actor Ryan Gosling created a Vine account for the sole purpose of creating a tribute

Vine in McHenry's honor. In the tribute, the actor poured a bowl of cereal and ate a spoonful of it while staring at the camera. He did this because McHenry had spent over a year creating funny Vines where he attempted to "feed" Ryan Gosling a spoonful of cereal through a video screen. These film clips were timed perfectly to make it look as though Gosling was refusing to eat his cereal (See Figure 8.2).

McHenry continued to make and post these funny Vines throughout his battle with cancer and the aggressive treatments he endured. Interspersed between shots from his treatments and other short clips were the "Ryan Gosling Won't Eat His Cereal" Vines. Gosling's posthumous tribute to McHenry occurred only online. As an example of

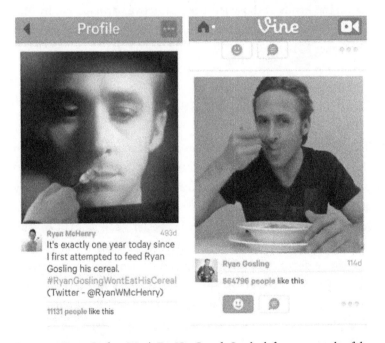

Figure 8.2 Ryan Gosling Won't Eat His Cereal. On the left, one example of the posts that McHenry made. On the right, Gosling's tribute Vine posted after McHenry's death.

a digital legacy, the virtual veneration reminds us that as we prepare for death and what we leave behind, we may generate a presence that is only acknowledged fully online.

Future research should investigate the possibility that while the virtual may come to augment and support what is occurring in the actual, there may also be virtual online mourning experiences that have no representation in ontological reality. The culmination of the hybridization of our consciousness through the virtual and the actual can be something that we pursue in an attempt to live forever. It is not beyond the awareness of most mobile media users that the actions we take in the everyday leave digital traces. The ways in which this digital clutter can become significant may rest in the hands of those left behind. Active participation by others is still often required for our digital legacies to be maintained (Brubaker 2016).

MOBILE WITNESSING AND ITS AFFECT

The witnessing relationship to an image's affect is heightened in the case of mobile media. Victims as well as psychopaths have used mobile media during events to create a heighted sense of intimacy and co-presence. Digital legacies have the potential to take on a horrific quality. On August 26, 2015, Vester Lee Flanagan II, who went by the pseudonym of Bryce Williams, initiated a fatal shooting that he documented fully through the use of packaged media as well as UCC. Flanagan was a journalist. As a gay African American man, he claimed that he experienced workplace discrimination at multiple places of employment, the last being the television station WDBJ in Roanoke, Virginia (US). During his time at WDBJ, he had negative interactions with the management of the station, as well as with the reporter Alison Parker (who at the time was an intern) and cameraman Adam Ward. He was subsequently fired from his position, a move that Flanagan interpreted as both retaliatory and discriminatory.

It was the widely publicized, racially motivated, mass shooting in an African American church in Charleston, South Carolina (US), on June 17, 2015, by a white supremacist, Dylann Roof, that served as Flanagan's tipping point for seeking his own brand of justice in response to his perceived victimization. He methodically planned his action against the news station and the targeted employees, Parker and Ward. He planned to leave a digital legacy of his mayhem by using what he knew about mainstream media news outlets and packaged media, as well as his ability to use social media platforms to distribute information and control its content and narrative.

Flanagan planned to commit the shooting during a live, on-location TV broadcast in the early morning hours. Even though he knew the shooting would be captured and broadcast live, Flanagan also wore a bodycam to document the shooting from his own perspective. Since the shooting was broadcast live through the news station, it did not take long for it to become *the* news. Once Flanagan knew that national news outlets had acknowledged the shooting, he faxed a manifesto/suicide note to a major national news network.

After his name was released nationally as Bryce Williams via mainstream media, Flanagan made his own Twitter account (@ bryce_williams7) public. Via his mobile device, he began to live-tweet his justification for the shooting while leaving the scene of the crime. His Twitter profile had been pristinely constructed prior to the event, as a quasi-memorial page with a profile picture of his time as a newscaster and personal photographs of himself at various stages in this life, from infancy through adulthood (See Figure 8.3). One can only imagine the validation he felt as people began to follow him

Figure 8.3 Screenshot of Bryce Williams's Twitter feed.

and retweet his tweets. As Farhad Manjoo reported in the *New York Times* (August 26 2015),

> There was initially some doubt on Twitter about the authenticity of the killer's account—justified skepticism, because the quickly pulled-together profile of a shooter has also become a hallmark of the ritual in which these incidents are covered. But then the killer's account, @bryce_williams7, began updating live, erasing

all doubt. Over the course of 20 minutes on Twitter, the shooter updated his status a half-dozen times, culminating in a post showing the video of the killings. He quickly amassed a following of thousands, the sort of rapturous social media welcoming that is usually reserved for pop stars and heads of state.

In one of his tweets, Flanagan posted a link to the video he recorded of the shootings on Facebook. This video is from his perspective. The camera's eye is in line with the raising of his weapon. After the first initial shots and the glimpse of horror in Alison Parker's face, the screen goes black. The accompanying audio provides an auditory account of the shooting. The video and the social media postings from Flanagan were about preserving his perspective and about having those who "visit" share in his understanding and his viewpoint (literally). His tweets and posts were then reposted and retweeted by thousands. It was not long before law enforcement was able to track his whereabouts. The digital tracking by authorities, facilitated in part by Flanagan's use of mobile media, became less of a chase and more of a lure for Flanagan. As a police officer approached his vehicle, Flanagan took his own life.

Despite Twitter's and Facebook's quick attempts to deactivate his social media accounts, Flanagan's digital legacy endures through screenshots, shared videos, and a mix of mainstream and citizen reporting.

The immediacy of mobile media was featured during the unfolding of the tragic shooting that took place on "Latin Night" in the LGBTQ club PULSE, in Orlando, Florida (US), on June 12, 2016. Almost instantaneously, news media outlets turned to people's social media pages to gather candid photos of the confirmed deceased and to construct their obituaries through public information shared on their Facebook pages and other sites. Survivors and loved ones were featured for their ability to give an "inside look" into the scene of the crime through what their loved one's had texted or through what they had posted on social media from inside the club during the shooting. There seemed to be no criticism of or hesitation in sharing the details in the name of protecting the deceased's privacy.

Both the victims' and the shooter's use of mobile media were on display. First images of the shooter were selfies taken from his social media page. Details about the events of the night were brought into startling revelation through screen shots of text messages, captured Snapchat videos, and personal cell phone video. Victims of the shooting were texting and posting from inside the club during the three-hour standoff with the shooter. In the hours after the standoff ended—when the crime scene was secured and the dead remained inside for investigation purposes—investigators and first responders were haunted by the constant ringing of the cell phones of the dead. This reality of the new ritual of phoning the dead became a chilling phenomenon spread on social media and reacted to by thousands, as many people posted about it after hearing from a first responder on CNN (see Figure 8.4). These new rituals function at the edge of consciousness and in the disbelief of loss.

In the days following the incident, much digital content coming from survivors and friends was used to recreate the scene of the crime. Here mobile media's role as witness and as witnessing became prevalent. The Snapchat selfie video of Amanda Alvear relives the mundanity of dancing with friends being quickly interrupted by unfamiliar gunshots. The tragic feelings of a mother's loss of her son were vividly captured by the disseminated text messages Eddie Jamoldroy Justice sent to his mother while hiding in the toilet from the gunman. It was Eddie's call to his mother that in turn made her call 911 and alert them to the terrifying events unfolding. As the events happened, Eddie continued to relay text messages between himself and his mother until he was killed. In these text messages

Andy Carvin
June 12 at 8:53am · 🌐

RE: the Orlando shooting, CNN just described something I've never thought of - as investigators are inside the nightclub, where many of the bodies are still where they fell, they have to tune out the nightmarish sound of all of the deceased phones' ringing constantly as loved ones try to reach them. #shudder

👍 Like   💬 Comment   ➴ Share

😮🙂😢 Michael A. Thill and 30K others   Top Comments ▾

44,091 shares

Write a comment...   📷 ☺

I think even just that description of this scene is going to haunt me.
Like · Reply · 👍 5,335 · June 12 at 12:25pm

Figure 8.4 Screenshot of Andy Carvin's Facebook post.

the feelings of fear, love, and death are compressed into the etiquette of the medium.

Through the dissemination of mobile media fragments by the deceased just before being shot, a particular kind of intimate public affect was made palpable. The deceased were then memorialized by strangers via social media. These mobile media eulogies speak of a new type of punctum, a new mobile affect. The candid and personal photos of the deceased made it easy for perfect strangers to become part of the witnessing process, and thus also be deeply affected and impacted by the loss. Not unlike the Sewol ferry disaster, these losses were politicized for the shooter's desire to target a gay nightclub and for his pledge of allegiance to the Islamic State (terrorist organization). A member of the US House of Representatives read the text messages between Eddie Justice and his mother on the House floor on June 22, 2016, in an effort to force the House to vote on gun control measures. Images of the deceased were turned into memes and have been used to mobilize millions of people and intimate publics. Selfies of the deceased were also used to create a tangible memorial at the site of the shooting (See Figure 8.5).

The public is left with the question of what to do with digital legacies of this sort. What does it mean when people share and repurpose this kind of content? The benign and even "friendly" environments of SNS become vulnerable to the infusion of the grotesque and the profane. Advances in features aimed at increasing the enjoyment and ease of the use of media-rich sites can become features used to spread terror and trauma. Moreover, in this documenting and sharing of tragedy, the unevenness of bodies is highlighted. Some bodies are more "mournable" or "grievable"—age, ethnicity, class, and sexual orientation all feed into this unspoken biopolitic. The video

Figure 8.5 Collages of selfies used to create real-time memorial at site of Pulse nightclub shooting (Cumiskey's personal photo).

"autoplay" feature now on many social media and digital media sites has the potential to expose a vulnerable public to graphic content.

Live broadcasts, not unlike the broadcast of Philando Castile's murder, are also risky in their ability to capture death and its impact online. One key example of this phenomenon is Anthony (Tony) Perkins. The 28-year-old man was broadcasting live from his neighborhood in Chicago, Illinois (US). It was a warm evening in June 2016, and he is seen drinking some Hennessey cognac. It is a regular mundane event: hanging out with his friends in front of his house. During the live Facebook broadcast, he makes furtive glances towards the camera of his phone as he reads and responds to what people are posting live, and then he looks away from his phone as he interacts with friends present and scans his neighborhood.

A quiet moment elapses as Tony looks off into the distance, perhaps attempting to make himself more aware of his surroundings. Those of us watching are facing him, so we do not see what he sees. Even when he is taken by surprise by a hail of bullets, the camera continues to roll. The image blurs as Tony begins to run. We catch a glimpse of blood and bloodstained grass, and then screams as Tony is still moving around—now on the ground with people shouting "Call the police!" Then the screen goes black but we can still hear the chaos around him. A female voice exclaims frantically in the darkness, "You good Tony, you good," in attempts to reassure him. We are unsure whether he is alive or dead at this point.

Paramedics arrive on the scene and his phone begins ringing over and over again. This automatic exposure to objectionable material can harm the psyche of viewers, despite any efforts to warn users of the nature of the content, and especially when it occurs without warning. Research around the role of witnessing and the ethics of disseminating troubled images continues in fields of memorialization and memory studies. As Papailias (forthcoming) notes, the rise of "trigger warnings" often involves certain types of bodies that create specific types of mourning socialities. As she notes in the case of online remediation of images of the dead body of the three-year-old Kurdish-Syrian refugee Alan Kurdi, and the associated "necropolitics," certain bodies have the right to be mourned in public, but others don't. She questions who gives the rights to mourn, and asks why some bodies are more grievable than others. "Grievability" is not a given—rather, it is "unevenly distributed: not all lives are recognized as valuable and thus in death treated as a loss to be mourned." The biopolitics of the unevenness of networked dead bodies and their affect in terms of mourning socialities is an area in need of increasing critique by the likes of Papailias.

SHIFTING CULTURAL UNDERSTANDINGS OF DEATH: A MOBILE-EMOTIVE AFTERLIFE

In *Haunting Hands* we have provided examples of the "reanimation" aspect of after-death, mobile-mediated communication, and how mobile social media can facilitate a digital afterlife—especially if digital legacies mean that our lives and legends are extended electronically. Mobile media allow for users to affectively transcend physical reality and foster a "theater of the mind." Recurring observations in the data involve struggles with the theatrics of keeping a loved one "alive" through mobile media. While bodies might be gone, memories and co-presence can be extended through the use of mobile media. Paradoxically, through engaging in mobile-emotive rituals of resurrecting via remembering our loved ones, we are still made aware through encounters with practical reality, that our loved ones really are dead.

In this concluding chapter, we have highlighted some of the future areas for mobile media memorialization. By discussing a few key areas, we hope these propositions—such as more longitudinal and comparative methods, along with interrogating why some bodies are more mournable and the politics of managing digital data of the dead—will be taken on by future researchers. These areas need new, revised, and interdisciplinary methods that account for cultural and generational differences. While users may engage in the co-creation of a shared online space where their loved ones "live on"—as evidenced in our data—users also generate a private space between themselves and their devices, within which they enter a virtual realm of seemingly eternal connection. These mobile devices are carried with the person and have the potential to augment and overlay everyday experiences with co-created digital reality and mobile-emotive co-presence.

The treasured artifact we carry with us can connect us to others and provide an ambiguous medium through which we can construct and co-construct personal narratives and expanded representations of self and our relationship to others. However, this device is also a private place, an intimate space. This virtual yet intimate world has the potential to enter physical reality.

Mobile technology is becoming more than wireless—it is wearable, ethereal, second skin, and second surface. These wireless technologies are hovering in and around many facets of everyday life, often unflinchingly. The movement toward wireless technologies and seemingly seamless modes of co-presence also creates new seams of boundaries and limits (Cumiskey and Hjorth 2013). Mobile technology has a history in paradoxical modes; as Arnold notes, mobile technologies are Janus-faced—they "set us free" at the same time that they create new obligations (2003).

In amplifying the ability of death to make us question our social norms and values, mobile media memorialization has the ability to make death more than just an event—it also allows for the procedural nature of bereavement. Through mobile media, this extends traditional disciplinary approaches to death. Through the digital—and especially the mobile—these approaches to ritualization are in need of revision. This situation is also applicable for trajectories of mourning that traditional psychological models promote. Mobile-emotive grieving lends itself to the more narrative approaches to grief and brings into focus the idea that life is a series of continual losses, through which we negotiate an ongoing fluctuation between absence and presence.

Mobile-emotive devices make us more adaptable to these ebbs and flows of connection and disconnection. The promise of a digital legacy and an ability to extend our presence beyond the physical fulfills our desire to avoid death at all costs. What is to be gained or lost if death becomes irrelevant? Is it death that defines the meaning of life, or does the building of new imaginative forms of a digital existence now come to define our understanding of our purpose and ourselves?

Mobile-emotive technology has the potential to promote immortality as a digital continuity of our spirit and the spirit of our loved ones beyond death (Geraci 2010). Death itself, inextricably linked to life, has much to teach us about mobile media and the role that it plays in the management of our deeply emotional and affective lives. Mobile-emotive devices offer us the opportunity to be simultaneously witness, participant, and subject to life events like never before. Life, death, and eternity may now reside in the palm of our hands.

BIBLIOGRAPHY

Ahmed, Sara. 2004. *The Cultural Politics of Emotion*. London: Routledge.

Ahmed, Sara. 2010. "Happy Objects." In *The Affect Theory Reader*, edited by M. Gregg and G. J. Seigworth, 29–51. Durham, NC: Duke University Press.

Ai, Amy L., Andreas Kastenmüller, Terrence N. Tice, Paul Wink, Michele Dillon, and Dieter Frey. 2014. "The Connection of Soul (COS) Scale: An Assessment Tool for Afterlife Perspectives in Different Worldviews." *Psychology of Religion and Spirituality* 6 (4): 316–29.

ALT. 2014. "Please Get Involved in Yellow Ribbon Campaign for Victims of Sewol Ferry Tragedy." Blog.Naver.com, April 21. http://m.blog.naver.com/alterlt/208493346.

Anderson, Benedict. 1982. *Imagined Communities*. New York: Verso.

Auslander, Phillip. 1999. *Liveness: Performance in a Mediatized Culture*. New York: Routledge.

Ariès, Philip. 1981. *The Hour of Our Death*. London: Allen Lane.

Arnold, Michael. 2004. "On the Phenomenology of Technology: The 'Janus-Faces' of Mobile Phones." *Information and Organization* 13: 231–56.

Bainbridge, William Sims. 2013. "Perspectives on Virtual Veneration." *The Information Society* 29 (3): 196–202.

Baker, Camille C. 2013. "MINDtouch: Embodied Mobile Media Ephemeral Transference." *Leonardo* 46 (3): 221–224.

Baron, Naomi. 2010. *Always On*. Oxford: Oxford University Press.

Barstow, Cheri. 2010. "What Is Channeling?" ElementallySpeaking.com. Accessed July 19, 2015. http://www.elementallyspeaking.com/channeling.html.

Barthes, Roland. 1981. *Camera Lucida*. New York: Farrar, Straus and Giroux.

BBC 2014. "Korea Ferry: News Conference." BBC.com. Accessed April 18, 2014. http://www.bbc.com/news/world-asia-27062348.

Bell, Catherine. 1992. *Ritual Theory, Ritual Practice*. New York: Oxford University Press.

Bennett, Gillian, and Kate Mary Bennett. 2000. "The Presence of the Dead: An Empirical Study." *Mortality* 5 (2): 139–57. doi:10.1080/13576270050076795.

Berlant, Lauren. 1998. "Intimacy: A Special Issue." *Critical Inquiry* 24 (2): 281–88.

Bollmer, Grant. 2012. "Demanding Connectivity: The Performance of 'True' Identity and the Politics of Social Media." *JOMEC Journal* 1: 1–13. http://www.cardiff.ac.uk/jomec/jomecjournal/1june2012/bollmer connectivity.pdf.

Bollmer, Grant. 2013. "Millions Now Living Will Never Die: Cultural Anxieties about the Afterlife of Information." *The Information Society* 29 (3): 142–51.

Bollmer, Grant. 2015. "Fragile Storage, Archival Futures." *Journal of Contemporary Archaeology* 2 (1): 66–72.

Bolter, David Jay, and Richard Grusin. 1999. *Remediation*. Cambridge, MA: MIT Press.

Bourdieu, Pierre. (1979) 1984. *Distinctions*. Cambridge, MA: Harvard University Press.

Bowlby, John. 1980. *Attachment and Loss*, Vol. 3, *Loss, Sadness, and Depression*. New York: Basic Books.

boyd, danah m., and Nicole B. Ellison. 2007. "Social Network Sites: Definition, History, and Scholarship." *Journal of Computer-Mediated Communication* 13 (1): 210–30. doi:10.1111/j.1083-6101.2007.00393.x.

Brubaker, Jed. 2016. "Stewarding Someone Else's Self: A Study of Stewardship Experiences of Post-mortem Profiles on Facebook." Paper presented at the International Communication Association Annual Conference in Fukuoka, Japan, June 13.

Brubaker, Jed, and Gillian Hayes. 2011. "A Study of Post-mortem Social Networking." Paper presented at the 2011 Workshop on Ubiquitous Computing Uniting the Californias, Ensenada, Mexico, March 3–5.

Brubaker, Jed R., Gillian R. Hayes, and Paul Dourish. 2013. "Beyond the Grave: Facebook as a Site for the Expansion of Death and Mourning." *The Information Society: An International Journal* 29 (3): 152–63. doi: 10.1080/01972243.2013.777300.

Brubaker, Jed, Funda Kivran-Swaine, Lee Taber, and Gillian Hayes. 2012. "Grief-Stricken in a Crowd: The language of bereavement and distress in social media." In *Proceedings of ICWSM-12*, Dublin, Ireland, June 4–8.

Bruns, Axel, Jean Burgess, Kate Crawford, and Frances Shaw. 2012. *#qldfloods and @QPSMedia: Crisis Communication on Twitter in the 2011 South East Queensland Floods*. Brisbane: ARC Centre of Excellence for Creative Industries and Innovation.

Bunbury, Stephanie. 2014. "Finding Vivian Maier Documentary, Exhibition Shine Light on a Late-Developing Photographer." *Sydney Morning Herald*, October 3, 2014. Accessed October 3, 2014. http://www.smh.com.au/entertainment/movies/finding-vivian-maier-documentary-exhibition-shine-light-on-a-latedeveloping-photographer-20141001-10oc1d.html.

Butler, Lisa. 2007. "Electronic Voice Phenomena as Evidence for Life after Death." *Journal of Spirituality & Paranormal Studies* 30 (July): 129–34.

Carroll, Evan, and John Romano. 2011. *Your Digital Afterlife*. Berkeley, CA: New Riders.

Chalfen, Richard. 2008. "Shinrei Shashin: Photographs of Ghosts in Japanese Snapshots." *Photography and Culture* 1 (1): 51–71. doi:10.2752/175145108784861428.

Choi, I. S., and S. H. Kwak. 2014. '"I Really Want To Live . . . The Temperature of My Brain Is 100 Degrees': Another Disclosed Video Was Found." *Oh My News*. Accessed July 18, 2014. http://www.ohmynews.com/NWS_Web/View/at_pg.aspx?CNTN_CD=A0002014660.

Choi, I. Y. 2014. "Breaking News: Funeral Parade in Honour of the Deceased Filled the Online Memorial Altar." *Yonhap News*, April 4. http://www.yonhapnews.co.kr/bulletin/2014/04/24/0200000000AKR20140424151500017.HTML.

Church, Scott H. 2013. "Digital Gravescapes: Digital Memorializing on Facebook." *The Information Society: An International Journal* 29 (3): 184–89. doi:10.1080/01972243.2013.777309.

CNN Staff. 2014. "'Please Hurry'—Transcript of Sinking Ferry's Desperate Calls Released." CNN News, April 21. http://edition.cnn.com/2014/04/18/world/asia/south-korea-ferry-transcript/index.html.

Code, Pamela, and Larry Poston. 2015. "Not Going Gentle into That Good Night: Science and Religion in the Face of Death." *Journal of Religion, Spirituality & Aging* 27 (1): 67–86.

Cooke, Grayson, and Amanda Reichelt-Brushett. 2015. "Archival Memory and Dissolution the After Image Project." *Convergence: The International Journal of Research into New Media Technologies* 21 (1): 8–26.

Corless, Inge B., Rana Limbo, Regina Szylit Bousso, Robert L. Wrenn, David Head, Norelle Lickiss, and Hannelore Wass. 2014. "Languages of Grief: A Model for Understanding the Expressions of the Bereaved." *Health Psychology and Behavioral Medicine: An Open Access Journal* 2 (1): 132–43.

Cumiskey, Kathleen M. 2005. "'Surprisingly Nobody Tried to Caution Her': Perceptions of Intentionality and the Role of Social Responsibility in the Public Use of Mobile Phones." In *Mobile Communications: Re-Negotiation of the Social Sphere*, edited by Rich Ling and Per Pedersen, 225–36. London: Springer.

Cumiskey, Kathleen M., and Larissa Hjorth, eds. 2013. *Mobile Media Practices, Presence and Politics: The Challenge of Being Seamlessly Mobile*. New York: Routledge.

Cumiskey, Kathleen M., and Rich Ling. 2015. "The Social Psychology of Mobile Communication." In *The Handbook of the Psychology of Communication Technology*, edited by S. Shyam Sundar, 228–46. Chichester, UK: John Wiley & Sons.

Currier, Joseph M., Jennifer E. F. Irish, Robert A. Neimeyer, and Joshua D. Foster. 2015. "Attachment, Continuing Bonds, and Complicated Grief Following Violent Loss: Testing a Moderated Model." *Death Studies* 39 (4): 201–210. doi:10.1080/07481187.2014.975869.

Davis, Erik. 1998. *TechGnosis: Myth, Magic and Mysticism in the Age of Information*. New York: Harmony Books.

Daggett, Luann M. 2005. "Continued Encounters: The Experience of After-Death Communication." *Journal of Holistic Nursing* 23 (2): 191–207.

D'Amore, Salvatore, and Lidia Scarciotta. 2011. "Los(t)s in Transitions: How Diverse Families Are Grieving and Struggling to Achieve a New Identity." *Journal of Family Psychotherapy* 22 (1): 46–55.

Dannenbaum, Sandra M., and Richard T. Kinnier. 2009. "Imaginal Relationships with the Dead Applications for Psychotherapy." *Journal of Humanistic Psychology* 49 (1): 100–113.

de Souza e Silva, Adriana, and Larissa Hjorth. 2009. "Urban Spaces as Playful Spaces." *Simulation & Gaming* 40 (5): 602–25.

de Vries, Brian, and Jane Rutherford. 2004. "Memorializing Loved Ones on the World Wide Web." *Omega: Journal of Death and Dying* 49 (1): 5–26.

Deger, Jennifer. 2006. *Shimmering Screens*. Minneapolis: Minnesota University Press.

Deger, Jennifer. 2008. "Imprinting on the Heart." *Visual Anthropology* 21 (4): 292–309.

Derrida, Jacques, and Bernard Stiegler. 2002. *Echographies of Television: Filmed Interviews*. Translated by Jennifer Bajorek. Malden, MA: Polity Press.

Doka, Kenneth J., ed. 2002. *Disenfranchised Grief: New Directions, Challenges, and Strategies for Practice*. Champaign, IL: Research Press.

Doran, Gerry, and Nancy Downing Hansen. 2006. "Constructions of Mexican American Family Grief after the Death of a Child: An Exploratory Study." *Cultural Diversity and Ethnic Minority Psychology* 12(2): 199–211.

Drewry, M. Damaris. 2003. "Purported After-Death Communication and Its Role in the Recovery of Bereaved Individuals: A Phenomenological Study." In *Proceedings of the Annual Conference of the Academy of Religion and Psychical Research*, 74–87. Bloomfield, CT: Academy of Religion and Psychical Research.

Durkheim, Émile. (1951) 1897. *Suicide*. London: Simon & Schuster.

Dutton, William H., and Frank Nainoa. 2002. Say Goodbye . . . Let's Roll: The Social Dynamics of Wireless Networks on September 11. *Prometheus* 20 (3): 237–45.

Edmonds, John W., and George T. Dexter. 1853. *Spiritualism*. New York: Partridge & Brittan.

Ernst, Wolfgang. 2012. *Digital Memory and the Archive*, (ed) Jussi Parrika. Minnesota: University of Minnesota Press.

ESCAP (Economic and Social Commission for Asia and the Pacific). 2015. *National Disasters in Asia and the Pacific: 2014 Year in Review*. New York: United Nations. http://www.unescap.org/news/enhanced-regional-cooperation-key-building-resilience-floods-and-landslides.

Fabian, Johannes. (1973) 2004. "How Others Die: Reflections on the Anthropology of Death." In *Death, Mourning and Burial: A cross-cultural reader*, edited by Antonius C. G. M. Robben, 49–61. Oxford: Blackwell.

Farman, Jason 2011. *Mobile Interface Theory*. London: Routledge.

Fortunati, Leopoldina. 2002. "The Mobile Phone: Towards New Categories and Social Relations." *Information, Communication & Society* 5 (4): 513–28.

Freud, Sigmund. (1917) 1973. "Mourning and Melancholia." In *The Standard Edition of the Complete Psychological Works of Sigmund Freud*. Vol. 14. Translated by James Strachey, 243–58. London: Hogarth Press.

Frohlich, David, Allan Kuchinsky, Celine Pering, Abbe Don, and Steven Ariss. 2002. "Requirements for Photoware." In *CSCW'02: Proceedings of the 2002 ACM Conference on Computer Supported Cooperative Work*, 166–75. New York: ACM Press.

Frosh, Paul. 2001. "The Public Eye and the Citizen-Voyeur: Photography as a Performance of Power." *Social Semiotics* 11 (1): 43–59.

Frosh, Paul. 2015. "The Gestural Image: The Selfie, Photography Theory, and Kinesthetic Sociability." *International Journal of Communication* 9: 1607–1628.

Geraci, Robert. 2010. *Apocalyptic AI: Visions of Heaven in Robotics, Artificial Intelligence and Virtual Reality*. New York: Oxford University Press.

Gibbs, Martin, Tamara Kohn, Bjorn Nansen, and Michael Arnold. 2015a. (DP140101871) *Digital Commemoration: Commemorative Practices, Digital Platforms, and Social Formations*. Australian Research Council (ARC) Discovery Project.

Gibbs, Martin, James Meese, Michael Arnold, Bjorn Nansen, and Marcus Carter. 2015b. "#Funeral and Instagram: Death, Social Media, and Platform Vernacular." *Information, Communication & Society* 18 (3): 255–68. doi:10.1080/1369118X. 2014.987152.

Gibson, Margaret. 2008. *Objects of the Dead*. Melbourne: Melbourne University Press.

Gibson, Margaret. 2014. "Digital Objects of the Dead: Negotiating Electronic Remains." In *The Social Construction of Death: Interdisciplinary Perspectives*, edited by Leen Van Brussel and Nico Carpentier, 221–38. Basingstoke: UK: Palgrave Macmillan.

Gibson, Margaret. 2015. "Automatic and Automated Mourning: Messengers of Death and Messages from the Dead." *Continuum* 29 (3), 339–53.

Gill, Tom, Brigitte Steger, and David H. Slater. 2013. *Japan Copes with Calamity*. New York: Peter Lang.

Goffman, Erving. (1957) 2005. *Interaction Ritual: Essays in Face to Face Behavior*. New York: Aldine Transaction.

Goggin, Gerard. 2006. *The Cell Culture*. New York: Routledge.

Goggin, Gerard. 2011. *Global Mobile Media*. New York: Routledge.

Goggin, Gerard, and Larissa Hjorth, eds. 2009. *Mobile Technologies*. New York: Routledge.

Google Play Shop. 2014. "Yellow Ribbon Campaign Application." Accessed April 25, 2014. https://play.google.com/store/apps/details?id=com.YellowRibbon.Campaign&hl=ko.

Gotved, Stine. 2014. Research Review: Death Online—Alive and Kicking! *Thanatos* 3 (1).https://thanatosjournal.files.wordpress.com/2012/12/gotved_deathonline2.pdf.

Gordon, Avery F. 2001. *Ghostly Matters: Haunting and the Sociological Imagination*. Minneapolis: University of Minnesota Press.

Gordon, Eric, and Adriana de Souza e Silva,. 2011. *Net Locality*. Chichester, UK: Wiley-Blackwell.

Graham, Conor, Michael Arnold, Tamara Kohn, and Martin R. Gibbs. 2015. "Gravesites and Websites: A Comparison of Memorialisation." *Visual Studies* 30 (1): 37–53. doi: 10.1080/1472586X.2015.996395.

Graham, Conor, Martin Gibbs, and Lanfranco Aceti. 2013. "Introduction to the Special Issue on the Death, Afterlife, and Immortality of Bodies and Data." *The Information Society* 29 (3): 133–41. doi:10.1080/ 01972243.2013.777296.

Gregg, Melissa. 2011. *Work's Intimacy*. London: Polity Press.

Guggenheim, Bill, and Judy Guggenheim. 1997. *Hello from Heaven*. New York: Bantam.

Gutierrez, Cathy. 2003. "From Electricity to Ectoplasm: Hysteria and American Spiritualism." *Aries* 3 (1): 55–81. doi:10.1163/15700590360472669.

Hagenmaier, Emily Boone. 2009. "'Untitled' (Queer Mourning and the Art of Felix Gonzalez-Torres)." *At the Interface/Probing the Boundaries* 58 (April): 157–67.

Hall, Christopher. 2001. "Reconstructing Meaning in the Wake of Loss: Creating 'Meaning Full' Ritual." *Grief Matters* 4 (3): 51–53.

Hand, Martin. 2013. *Ubiquitous Photography*. New York: John Wiley & Sons.

Hansen, Bjorn, Martin Gibbs, Michael Arnold, and Tamara Kohn. 2014. "Selfies at Funeral." Paper presented at the Association of Internet Researchers Conference, October, South Korea.

Hansen, Mark B. N. 2006. *Bodies in Code: Interfaces with Digital Media*. New York: Routledge.

Harper, Mairi, Rory O'Connor, Adele Dickson, and Ronan O'Carroll. 2011. "Mothers Continuing Bonds and Ambivalence to Personal Mortality after the Death of Their Child—An Interpretative Phenomenological Analysis." *Psychology, Health & Medicine* 16 (2): 203–14.

Hastings, Arthur. 2012. "Effects of Bereavement Using a Restrictive Sensory Environment." *Journal of Transpersonal Psychology* 44 (1): 2–25.

Haverinen, Anna. 2014. "Death and Mourning Rituals in Online Environments." PhDdiss., University of Turku.

Hendry, Natalie. 2016. *Visualising Recovery*. PhDdiss., RMIT University.

Hertz, Robert. (1907) 1960. *Death and the Right Hand*. New York: Free Press.

Hjorth, Larissa. 2005. "Postal Presence: The Persistence of the Post Metaphor in Current SMS/MMS Practices." In "Mobilities, New Social Intensities and the Coordinates of Digital Networks." Special issue, *Fibreculture Journal* 6. http://journal.fibreculture.org/issue6/.

Hjorth, Larissa, and Michael Arnold. 2013. *Online@Asia-Pacific*. London: Routledge.

Hjorth, Larissa, and Kyoung-hwa Yonnie Kim. 2011a. "Good Grief: the Role of Social Mobile Media in the 3.11 Earthquake Disaster in Japan." *Digital Creativity Journal* 22 (3): 187–99.

Hjorth, Larissa, and Kyoung-hwa Yonnie Kim. 2011b. "The Mourning After: A Case Study of Social Media in the 3.11 Earthquake Disaster in Japan." *Television & New Media Journal* 12 (6): 552–59.

Hjorth, Larissa, and Sun Sun Lim. 2012. "Mobile Intimacy in the Age of Affective Mobile Media." *Feminist Media Studies* 12 (4): 477–84.

Hoskins, Andrew. 2011. "Media, Memory, Metaphor: Remembering and the Connective Turn." *Parallax,* 17 (4): 19–31.

Horst, Heather, and Daniel Miller. 2006. *The Cell Phone*. London: Berg.

Horton, Helen. 2015. "Selfie Deaths Are Now More Common Than Shark Attacks." *The Telegraph*, September 22, 2015. http://www.telegraph.co.uk/technology/11881900/More-people-have-died-by-taking-selfies-this-year-than-by-shark-attacks.html.

Huhtamo, Erkki, and Jussi Parikka. 2011. *Media Archaeology*. Berkeley: University of California Press.

Ito, Mizuko. 2003. "Mobiles and the Appropriation of Place." *Receiver* 8. Accessed December 10, 2005. http://academic.evergreen.edu/curricular/evs/readings/itoShort.pdf.

Ito, Mizuko, and Daisuke Okabe. 2005. "Intimate Visual Co-Presence." Paper presented at Ubicomp, Takanawa Prince Hotel, Tokyo, Japan, September 11–14. Accessed June 28th, 2006. http://www.itofisher.com/mito/.

Ito, Mizuko, Daisuke Okabe, and Misa Matsuda, eds. 2005. *Personal, Portable, Pedestrian*. Cambridge, MA: MIT Press.

Jenzen, Olu, and Sally R. Munt. 2013. *The Ashgate Research Companion to Paranormal Cultures*. Burlington, VT: Ashgate.

Jones, Steve. 2004. "404 Not Found: The Internet and the Afterlife." *Omega: Journal of Death and Dying* 49 (1): 83–88.

JTB News. 2014. "Came the Kakao Talk Messages When the Ferry was Sinking." Online video. Accessed April 16, 2014. http://news.jtbc.joins.com/article/article.aspx?news_id=NB10465003.

Kakao.com. 2014. Crystallization of Knowledge. Accessed 5 March 2015. https://story.kakao.com/ch/knowledge/jP3iJya7Nx0.

Kalan, Molly. 2015. "Expressions of Grief on Facebook: The Complicated Nature of Online Memorialization for the Bereaved." *Interface: Theorizing the Web* 1 (1). http://commons.pacificu.edu/cgi/viewcontent.cgi?article=1006&context=interface.

Kalish, Richard A., and David K. Reynolds. 1973. "Phenomenological Reality and Post-Death Contact." *Journal for the Scientific Study of Religion* 12 (2): 209–21.

Kasket, Elaine. 2012. "Being-towards-Death in the Digital Age." *Existential Analysis* 23 (2): 249–61.

Katz, James. 2006. *Magic in the Air*. Piscataway, NJ: Transaction.

Kearl, Michael. 1989. *Endings: A Sociology of Death and Dying*. New York: Oxford University Press.

Kember, Sarah, and Joanna Zylinska. 2012. *Life after New Media*. Cambridge, MA: MIT Press.

Kim, Luke Ik-Chang. 1996. "Korean Ethos." *Journal of Korean American Medical Association* 2 (1): 13–23.

Kim, Sung-hyun, and Soo-yong Jeon. 2014. "Ferry Captain Sentenced to 36 Years in Prison." *Chosun Ilbo*, November 12. http://english.chosun.com/site/data/html_dir/2014/11/12/2014111201226.html.

Kindberg, Tim, Mirjana Spasojevic, Rowanne Fleck, and Abigail Sellen,. 2005. "The Ubiquitous Camera: An In-Depth Study of Camera Phone Use." *IEEE Pervasive Computing* 4 (2), 42–50.

Klass, Dennis, Phyllis R. Silverman, and Steven L. Nickman. 1996. *Continuing Bonds: New Understandings of Grief*. New York: Routledge/Taylor & Francis.

Klassens, Mirjam, Peter Groote, and Frank Vanclay. 2013. "Expressions of Private Mourning in Public Space: The Evolving Structure of Spontaneous and Permanent Roadside Memorials in the Netherlands." *Death Studies* 37 (2): 145–71.

Klugman, Craig M. 2006. "Dead Men Talking: Evidence of Post Death Contact and Continuing Bonds." *Omega: Journal of Death & Dying* 53 (3): 249–62.

Kutz, Kimberly N. 2013. "Chief of a Nation of Ghosts: Images of Abraham Lincoln's Spirit in the Immediate Post–Civil War Period." *Journal of American Culture* 36 (2): 111–23.

Kwilecki, Susan. 2011. "Ghosts, Meaning and Faith: After-Death Communications in Bereavement Narratives." *Death Studies* 35: 219–43.

Lally, Elaine. 2002. *At Home with Computers*. Oxford and New York: Berg.

Lasén, Amparo. 2004. "Affective Technologies." *Receiver* 11. Accessed October 10, 2015. http://www.scribd.com/doc/142953400/Lasen-Amparo-2004-Affective-technologies#scribd.

Laursen, Ditte. 2013. "Organising 'My Mind Is with You': Continued Interaction after Closed Interaction via Mobile Phone." In *Mobile Media Practices, Presence and Politics: The Challenge of Being Seamlessly Mobile*, edited by Kathleen M. Cumiskey and Larissa Hjorth, 105–11. London: Routledge.

Lee, H. H., and J. H. Song. 2014. ' "I feel really scary. I want to live': Disclosed Video of Victims of Dan Won high School Was Found.' *Oh My News.* Accessed July 18, 2014. http://www.ohmynews.com/NWS_Web/view/at_pg.aspx?CNTN_ CD=A0002014649.

Lewis, Amy. 2015. "Selfie Deaths Are Now More Common Than Shark Attacks." *Stylist,* September 22. http://www.stylist.co.uk/life/selfie-deaths-are-now-more-common-than-shark-attacks-selfie-tips-advice.

Licoppe, Christian. 2004. "'Connected' Presence: The Emergence of a New Repertoire for Managing Social Relationships in a Changing Communication Technoscape." *Environmental and Planning D* 22 (1): 135–56.

Lim, Myoung-Soo. 2014. "Mum this might be the last chance to tell you, I love you mum." *Korea JoongAng Daily.* Accessed April 17, 2014. http://article.joins.com/ news/article/article.asp?total_id=14469894.

Lim, S. Y. 2014. "Does the yellow ribbon have copyright?" *DKB News (Dong A Ilbo),* April 22. http://news.donga.com/DKBNEWS/3/all/20140422/ 62958038/3.

Lin, Han, William Tov, and Lin Qiu. 2014. "Emotional Disclosure on Social Networking Sites: The Role of Network Structure and Psychological Needs." *Computers in Human Behavior* 41 (December): 342–50.

Ling, Richard. 2012. *Taken for Grantedness: The Embedding of Mobile Communication into Society.* Cambridge, MA: MIT Press.

Lingel, Jessa. 2013. "The Digital Remains: Social Media and Practices of Online Grief." *The Information Society: An International Journal* 29 (3): 190–95.

Lohmann, Roger Ivan. 2007. "Mementos of the Dead: Technologies of Memory Management in a New Guinea village" ("Souvenirs des morts: Techniques de gestion de la me´moire dans un village de Nouvelle-Guine´e"). *Journal de la Societe des Oceanistes* 124: 45–57.

Madianou, Mirca. "Humanitarian Technologies Project." European Research Council, 2013–2016.

Madianou, Mirca, and Daniel Miller. 2012. *Migration and New Media: Transnational families and Polymedia.* London: Routledge.

Manjoo, Farhad. 2015. "Virginia Shooting Gone Viral, in a Well-Planned Rollout on Social Media." *New York Times,* August 26. http://www.nytimes.com/2015/ 08/27/technology/personaltech/violence-gone-viral-in-a-well-planned-rollout-on-social-media.html.

Malinowski, Bronislaw. 2005. "Magic, Science and Religion." In *Death, Mourning and Burial: A Cross-Cultural Reader,* edited by Antonius C. G. M. Robben, 19–22. Oxford: Wiley-Blackwell.

Manovich, Lev. 2001. *The Language of New Media.* Cambridge, MA: MIT Press.

Manovich, Lev. 2003. "The Paradoxes of Digital Photography." In *The Photography Reader,* edited by Liz Wells, 240–49. New York: Routledge.

Mansour, Camille, and Leila Fawaz. 2009. *Transformed Landscapes: Essays on Palestine and the Middle East in Honor of Walid Khalidi*. Cairo, Egypt: American University in Cairo Press.

Marwick, Alice, and Nicole B. Ellison. 2012. "'There Isn't Wifi in Heaven!' Negotiating Visibility on Facebook Memorial Pages." *Journal of Broadcasting & Electronic Media* 56 (3): 378–400.

McKay, Deidre. 2012. *Global Filipinos: Migrants' Lives in the Virtual Village*. Bloomington: Indiana University Press.

McQuire, Scott. 2008. *The Media City*. London: SAGE.

Meikle, Graeme. 2011. *Media Convergence*. London: Palgrave Macmillan.

Mellos, Dimitri. 2013. "Unfrozen Moments: A Psychoanalytic Approach to the Uses of Photographs." *Psychoanalytic Psychology* 30 (2): 329–38.

Metcalf, Peter, and Richard Huntington. 1991. *Celebrations of Death: The Anthropology of Mortuary*. Cambridge, UK: Cambridge University Press.

Miller, Daniel, and Jolynna Sinanan. 2014. *Webcam*. London: Polity Press.

Milne, Esther. 2010. *Letters, Postcards, Email: Technologies of Presence*. New York: Routledge.

Mitchell, Lisa M., Peter H. Stephenson, Susan Cadell, and Mary Ellen Macdonald. 2012. "Death and Grief On-Line: Virtual Memorialization and Changing Concepts of Childhood Death and Parental Bereavement on the Internet." *Health Sociology Review* 21 (4): 413–31. doi:10.5172/hesr.2012.21.4.413.

Mitchell, Margaret. 2007. "Constructing Immortality: The Role of the Dead in Everyday Life." In *Remember Me: Constructing Immortality*, edited by Margaret Mitchell, 1–17. New York: Routledge/Taylor & Francis.

Moody, Raymond A. 1992. "Family Reunions: Visionary Encounters with the Departed in a Modern-Day Psychomanteum." *Journal of Near-Death Studies* 11 (2): 83–120.

Mullen, J. 2014. "Ferry Disaster: Yellow Ribbons Become Symbol of Hope, Solidarity." CNN News, April 24. http://edition.cnn.com/2014/04/24/world/asia/south-korea-yellow-ribbons/.

Murray-Parkes, Colin. 1975. *Bereavement*. Harmondsworth, UK: Penguin.

Nansen, Bjorn, Michael Arnold, Martin Gibbs, and Tamara Kohn. 2014. "The Restless Dead in the Digital Cemetery:" In *Digital Death: Mortality and Beyond in the Online Age*, edited by Christopher M. Moreman and A. David Lewis, 111–24. Santa Barbara: CA: ABC-CLIO.

Nansen, Bjorn, James Messe, Martin Gibbs, Michael Arnold, and Tamara Kohn. 2014. "Death and the Selfie: Welcome to a Grave New World." *The Conversation*, November 23. https://theconversation.com/death-and-the-selfie-welcome-to-a-grave-new-world-33687.

Neimeyer, Robert A. 2006. "Bereavement and the Quest for Meaning: Rewriting Stories of Loss and Grief." *Hellenic Journal of Psychology* 3: 181–88.

Neimeyer, Robert A, Dennis Klass, and Michael Robert Dennis. 2014. "A Social Constructionist Account of Grief: Loss and the Narration of Meaning." *Death Studies* 38 (8): 485–98. doi: 10.1080/07481187.2014.913454.

Palmer, Daniel. 2012. "iPhone Photography: Mediating Visions of Social Space." In *Studying Mobile Media: Cultural Technologies, Mobile Communication, and the iPhone*, edited by L. Hjorth, J. Burgess, and I. Richardson, 85–97. New York: Routledge.

Palmer, Daniel. 2014. "Mobile Media Photography." In *The Routledge Companion of Mobile Media*, edited by G. Goggin and L. Hjorth, 245–55. New York: Routledge.

Paquette, Danielle. 2016. "'This Is the Brain on Horror': The Incredible Calm of Diamond 'Lavish' Reynolds." *Washington Post*, July 7. https://www.washington-tonpost.com/news/wonk/wp/2016/07/07/the-incredible-calm-of-diamond-lavish-reynolds/.

Papailias, Penelope. 2016. "Witnessing in the Age of the Database: Viral Memorials, Affective Publics, and the Assemblage of Mourning." *Memory Studies* 9 (4): 437–54. DOI: 10.1177/1750698015622058

Papailias, Penelope. (forthcoming). "Haunting Europe: The (Un)Seeing of Dead Refugee Bodies." In *Death and Disposal*, edited by Tamara Kohn et al. London: Routledge.

Parikka, Jussi. 2013. *What Is Media Archaeology?* New York: John Wiley & Sons.

Partridge, Christopher. 2013. "Haunted Culture: The Persistence of Belief in the Paranormal." In *The Ashgate Research Companion to Paranormal Cultures*, edited by Olu Jenzen and Sally R. Munt, 39–50.Burlington, VT: Ashgate.

Pearce, Michael. 2011. "Accommodating the Discarnate: Thai Spirit Houses and the Phenomenology of Place." *Material Religion* 7 (3): 344–72.

Pertierra, Raul. 2006. *Transforming Technologies*. Manila, Philippines: De La Salle University Press.

Pertierra, Raul. 2013. "We Reveal Ourselves to Ourselves: The New Communication Media in the Philippines." *Social Science Diliman* 9 (1): 20–40.

Pertierra, Raul, Eduardo Ugarte, Alicia Pingol, Joel Hernandez, and Nikos Lexis Dacanay. 2002. *Txt-ing selves*. Manila, Philippines: De La Salle University Press.

Phillips, Patrick. 2009. *Boy*. Athens, GA: University of Georgia Press.

Qiu, Jack Linchuan. 2009. *Working-Class Network Society*. Cambridge, MA: MIT Press.

Raphael, Beverley. 2000. "Prevention in Psychiatry: Australian Contributions, Australian and New Zealand." *Journal of Psychiatry* 34 (November): S6–S13.

Reading, Anna. 2009a. "Memobilia: Mobile Phones Making New Memory Forms" In *Save As . . . Digital Memories*, edited by J. Garde-Hansen, A. Hoskins, and A. Reading, 81–95. Basingstoke, UK: Palgrave Macmillan.

Reading, Anna. 2009b. Mobile Witnessing: Ethics and the Camera Phone in the War on Terror. *Globalizations* 6 (1): 61–76

Refslund Christensen, Dorthe, and Stine Gotved. 2015. "Online Memorial Culture: An Introduction." *New Review of Hypermedia and Multimedia* 21(1–2): 1–9.

Refslund Christensen, Dorthe, and Kjetil Sandvik. 2014. *Mediating and Remediating Death*. London: Routledge.

Richardson, Kathleen, and Sue Hessey. 2009. "Archiving the Self? Facebook as Biography of Social and Relational Memory." *Journal of Information, Communication and Ethics in Society* 7 (1): 25–38.

Riley, Adam. 2012. "Spirit Camera: The Cursed Memoir (Nintendo 3DS Review)." Cubed3, August 7. http://www.cubed3.com/review/1129/1/spirit-camera-the-cursed-memoir-nintendo-3ds.html.

Robben, Antonius C. G. M. 2004. "Death and Anthropology: An Introduction." In *Death, Mourning and Burial: A Cross-Cultural Reader*, edited by Antonius C. G. M. Robben, 1–16. Oxford: Blackwell.

Roberts, Pamela. 2004. "The Living and the Dead: Community in the Virtual Cemetery." *Omega: Journal of Death & Dying* 49 (1): 57–76.

Rogers, Carl. 1980. *A Way of Being*. New York: Houghton Mifflin.

Rosenblatt, Paul C. 1995. "Ethics of Qualitative Interviewing with Grieving Families." *Death Studies* 19: 139–55.

Rosenblatt, Paul C. 1996. "Grief Does Not End." In *Continuing Bonds*, edited by Dennis Klass, Phyllis R. Silverman, and Steven L. Nickman. Washington, DC: Taylor & Francis.

Rosenblatt, Paul C. 2000. *Parent Grief*. Philadelphia: Brunner.

Rosenblatt, Paul C. 2008. "Grief across cultures." In *Handbook of Bereavement Research and Practice*, edited by Margaret S. Stroebe, Robert O. Hansson, Henk Schut, and Wolfgang Stroebe, 207–22. Washington, DC: American Psychological Association.

Rosaldo, Renato. 1989. "Introduction: Grief and a Headhunter's Rage." In *Culture and Truth: The Remaking of Social Analysis*, 1–21. Boston: Beacon Press.

Russac, R. J., Nina S. Steighner, and Angela I. Canto. 2002. "Grief Work versus Continuing Bonds: A Call for Paradigm Integration or Replacement?" *Death Studies* 26 (6): 463–78.

Saggaf, Yeslam al-, and Sharon Nielsen. 2014. "Self-Disclosure on Facebook among Female Users and Its Relationship to Feelings of Loneliness." *Computers in Human Behavior* 36 (July): 460–68.

Sanger, Michael. 2009. "When Clients Sense the Presence of Loved Ones Who Have Died." *Omega: Journal of Death & Dying* 59 (1): 69–89.

Schmalz, Dorothy L., Craig M. Colistra, and Katherine E. Evans. 2015. "Social Media Sites as a Means of Coping with a Threatened Social Identity." *Leisure Sciences* 37 (1): 20–38.

Schor, Esther H. 1994. *Bearing the Dead: The British Culture of Mourning from the Enlightenment to Victoria*. Princeton, NJ: Princeton University Press.

Sconce, Jeffrey. 2000. *Haunted Media: Electronic Presence from Telegraphy to Television.* Durham, NC: Duke University Press.

Segerstad, Ylva Af Hård, and D. Kasperowski. 2014. "A Community for Grieving: Affordances of Social Media for Support of Bereaved Parents." *New Review of Hypermedia and Multimedia* 21 (1–2): 25–41. doi: 10.1080/ 13614568.2014.983557.

Senft, Theresa, and Nancy Baym, 2015. "What Does the Selfie Say? Investigating a Global Phenomenon." *International Journal of Communication* 9: 1588–1606.

Sheller, Mimi. 2014. "Out of Your Pocket.", In *The Routledge Companion to Mobile Media,* edited by Gerard Goggin and Larissa Hjorth, 197–205. New York: Routledge.

Silverstone, Roger, and Leslie Haddon. 1996. "Design and the Domestication of ICTs: Technical Change and Everyday Life." In *Communication by Design: The Politics of Information and Communication Technologies,* edited by R. Silverstone and R. Mansell, 44–74. Oxford: Oxford University Press.

Sisainlive.com. Hyun-jin. 2014. Last Accessed on 10 June 2015. http://www.sisain-live.com/news/quickViewArticleView.html?idxno=20058.

Song, Hayeon, Anne Zmyslinski-Seelig, Jinyoung Kim, Adam Drent, Angela Victor, Kikuko Omori, and Mike Allen. 2014. "Does Facebook Make You Lonely?: A Meta Analysis." *Computers in Human Behavior* 36 (July): 446–52.

Sontag, Susan. 1977. *On Photography.* New York: Farrar, Straus and Giroux.

Spirit Guide Hai. 2006. Channeled by Paul McGlone. http://www.spiritsspeaking. com/okanagantrancemediumship.shtml.

"Spirits Speaking from the Heart at Tranquil Spirit—Public Demonstration of Spiritual Trance Mediumship/Channeling at Penticton, in the Okanagan, British Columbia, Canada, October 2006." Accessed July 17, 2015. http:// www.spiritsspeaking.com/okanagantrancemediumship.shtml.

Stanyek, Jason, and Benjamin Piekut. 2010. "Deadness Technologies of the Intermundane." *TDR: The Drama Review—A Journal of Performance Studies* 54 (1): 14–38.

Steinhart, Eric Charles. 2014. *Your Digital Afterlives.* New York: Palgrave Macmillan.

Sterne, Jonathan. 2003. *The Audible Past: Cultural Origins of Sound Reproduction.* Durham, NC: Duke University Press.

Stevens, Quentin. 2009. *The Ludic City.* London: Routledge.

Straight, Bilinda. 2010. "Death, Grief, and Cross-World Longing." *Reviews in Anthropology* 39 (2): 127–47.

Strathern, Marilyn. 1988. *The Gender of the Gift: Problems with Women and Problems with Society in Melanesia.* Berkeley: University of California Press.

Steffen, Edith, and Adrian Coyle. 2011. "Sense of Presence Experiences and Meaning-Making in Bereavement: A Qualitative Analysis." *Death Studies* 35 (7): 579–609.

Stroebe, Margaret, Henk Schut, and Wolfgang Stroebe. 2005. "Attachment in Coping with Bereavement: A Theoretical Integration." *Review of General Psychology* 9: 48–66

Suler, John. 2004. "The Online Disinhibition Effect." *CyberPsychology & Behavior* 7 (3): 321–26.

Suzuki, Hikaru. 2004. "The Phase of Negated Death." In *Death, Mourning and Burial: A Cross-Cultural Reader*, edited by Antonius C. G. M. Robben, 224–37. Oxford: Blackwell.

Sweeney, Kate. 2014. *American Afterlife: Encounters in the Customs of Mourning.* Athens, GA: University of Georgia Press.

Taylor, Alex, and Richard Harper 2002. "Age-Old Practices in the 'New World': A Study of Gift-Giving between Teenage Mobile Phone Users." In *Proceedings of the SIGCHI Conference on Human Factors in Computing Systems*, April 20–25, Minneapolis, Minnesota, 439-446. New York: ACM Press.

Turkle, Sherri. 2012. *Alone Together: Why We Expect More From Technology and Less From Each Other.* New York: Basic Books.

Turner, Phil. and Susan Turner. 2013. "Emotional and Aesthetic Attachment to Digital Artefacts." *Cognition, Technology & Work* 15: 403–14.

Unruh, David R. 1983. "Death and Personal History: Strategies of Identity Preservation." *Social Problems* 30 (3): 340–51.

Valentine, Christine. 2008. *Bereavement Narratives: Continuing Bonds in the Twenty-First Century.* Abingdon, Oxon, UK: Routledge.

Valentine, Christine. 2013. "Identity and Post-Mortem Relationships in the Narratives of British and Japanese Mourners." *Sociological Review* 61 (2): 383–401.

Van Boven, Leaf, Joanne Kane, A. Peter McGraw, and Jeannette Dale. 2010. "Feeling Close: Emotional Intensity Reduces Perceived Psychological Distance." *Journal of Personality and Social Psychology* 98 (6): 872–885.

van Dijck, José. 2007. *Mediated Memories in the Digital Age.* Stanford, CA: Stanford University Press.

van Gennep, Arnold. (1960) 2013. *The Rites of Passage.* New York: Routledge.

Van House, Nancy. 2011. "Personal Photography, Digital Technologies and the Uses of the Visual." *Visual Studies* 26 (2): 125–34.

Van House, Nancy, Marc Davis, Morgan Ames, Megan Finn and Vijay Viswanathan. 2005. "The Uses of Personal Networked Digital Imaging: An Empirical Study of Cameraphone Photos and Sharing." In *Proceedings of the SIGCHI Conference on Human Factors in Computing Systems*, April 2–7 Portland, Oregon. New York: ACM Press.

Veale, Kylie J. 2003. "A Virtual Adaptation of a Physical Cemetery for Diverse Researchers using Information Science Methods." *Computers in Genealogy* 8 (4): 16–38.

Veale, Kylie. 2004. "Online Memorialisation: The Web as a Collective Memorial Landscape for Remembering the Dead." *Fibreculture Journal* 3. http://three. fibreculturejournal.org/fcj-014-online-memorialisation-the-web-as-a-collective-memorial-landscape-for-remembering-the-dead/.

Verhoeff, Nanna. 2013. *Mobile Screens: The Visual Regime of Navigation.* Amsterdam: Amsterdam University Press.

Vincent, Jane. 2006. "Emotional Attachment and Mobile Phones," *Knowledge, Technology & Policy* 19 (1): 117–22.

Vincent, Jane. 2010. "Living with Mobile Phones." In *Mobile Media and the Change in Everyday Life,* edited by Joachim R. Höflich, Georg F. Kircher, Christine Linke, and Isobel Schlote, 155–170. Berlin: Peter Lang.

Vincent, Jane, and Leopoldina Fortunati, eds. 2009. *Electronic Emotion: The Mediation of Emotion via Information and Communication Technologies.* Oxford: Peter Lang.

Volkmer, Ingrid, ed. 2006. *News in Public Memory: An International Study of Media Memories across Generations.* New York: Peter Lang.

Walker Rettberg, Jill. 2014. *Seeing Ourselves through Technology.* London: Palgrave Pivot.

Wallace, Anthony F.C. 1966. *Religion: An Anthropological View.* New York: Random House.

Walter, Tony. 1996. *The Revival of Death.* London: Routledge.

Walter, Tony, Rachid Hourizi, Wendy Moncur, and Stacey Pitsillides. 2011. "Does the Internet Change How We Die and Mourn? Overview and Analysis." *Omega: Journal of Death and Dying* 64 (4): 275–302.

Wajcman, Judy. 2015. *Pressed for Time.* Chicago: Chicago University Press.

Wendt, Brooke. 2014. *The Allure of the Selfie.* Amsterdam: Institute of Network Cultures.http://networkcultures.org/wp-content/uploads/2014/10/The_Allure_ot_Selfie_los.pdf.

Wheeler-Roy, Susan, and Bernard A. Amyot. 2004. *Grief Counseling Resource Guide: A Field Manual.* New York: New York State Office of Mental Health.

Whittaker, Steve, Ofer Bergman, and Paul Clough. 2010. "Easy on That Trigger Dad: A Study of Long Term Family Photo Retrieval." *Personal and Ubiquitous Computing* 14 (1): 31–43.

Yonhap News. 2014. http://www.yonhapnews.co.kr/society/2014/04/30/07010 00000AKR2014 0430097351061.HTML.

YouTube. 2014. "The undisclosed last video filmed by a student." Accessed July 18, 2015. https://www.youtube.com/watch?v=FAbdIywTB7M.

YouTube, Dong Hyuk. 2014. Accessed June 10, 2015. https://www.youtube.com/watch?v=vUihH2NwAHA.

YouTube, Dong Hyuk Kim video. 2014. Accessed June 10, 2015. https://www.youtube.com/watch?v=vUihH2NwAHA.

YouTube, Parent's grief. 2014. Accessed June 10, 2015. http://www.youtube.com/watch?v=KrMyR-TEKS0.

YouTube, Si-yeon Kim video. 2014. Accessed June 10, 2015. https://www.youtube.com/watch?v=LM7lJYiYUI8&list=PLObZD1gF8d8XiKaJxWCeiMSuWHVFaqK9u.

YouTube, Ye-seul video. 2014. Accessed June 10, 2015. https://www.youtube.com/watch?v=dVEfPP8zLLc&index=2&list=PLObZD1gF8d8XiKaJxWCeiMSuWHVFaqK9u.

Zylinska, Joanna, ed. 2015. *Photomediations*. Open Humanities Press.

Zylinska, Joanna, and Sarah Kember. 2012. *Life after New Media*. Cambridge, MA: MIT Press.

INDEX

Italic page references are indicated for figures.

affect
  definition of, 27, 133, 186
  how mobile media amplifies, 3, 6, 26, 35,
    44, 140, 163, 178, 206, 208
  as punctum, 125
  social media and, 37, 87–88, 183
  witnessing, 7, 26, 147, 182, 195, 198, 203
affective. *See* affect
affective network, 147, 183
affirmation, rituals of, 20, 89–93, 97–98, 162
affordances
  mobile media, 3, 8, 10, 21, 55, 101, 126, 179
  networked technology/media, 135,
    180, 185
  social media, 59
after-death, 6, 127, 180, 184, 206
after-death communication (ADC), 21,
    37, 125, 144, 152, 163–68, 170,
    172, 174–75
afterlife
  cultural beliefs in, 37, 124, 179
  of data, 135
  definition of, 153–54
  mobile media and, 3, 4, 5, 6, 11, 37, 134,
    142, 148, 174, 178, 181, 206
Alvear, Amanda, 202
ancestor veneration avatars (AVA), 196
anthropology of death, 56–59

archives
  digital, 10, 104–7
  material, 104
artifacts
  digital, 12, 41, 81, 84, 88, 90–92, 103,
    105, 107
  material, 84, 90
artificial intelligence (AI), 190, 196
assumptive world, 89
attachment
  to mobile media, 25, 27, 83–84, 86,
    115, 190–91
  to others, 51, 58, 83, 100, 124, 155, 162
augmented reality (AR), 26, 131–32
automaticity of use, 189
avatars, 195–96

Barthes, Roland, 125, 146, 182
blocking, on social media, 69, 75, 110–11
broadcasting
  live, 14, 15, 125–26, 192, 199, 205
  mobile media, 8, 24, 36, 40, 79, 90, 92,
    148–49, 192

Camera Lucida, 146
camera phone, 4, 7, 10, 24, 49–50, 70, 91,
    124–25, 126–27, 131, 141, 146, 184
Castile, Philando, 192, 205

INDEX

CPSIA information can be obtained
at www.ICGtesting.com
Printed in the USA
BVHW01s2004081217
502079BV00001B/2/P